Stand Out 4

Standards-Based English

Second Edition

Staci Johnson

Rob Jenkins

HEINLE
CENGAGE Learning™

Australia • Brazil • Japan • Korea • Mexico • Singapore • Spain • United Kingdom • United States

HEINLE
CENGAGE Learning

**Stand Out 4: Standards-Based English,
Second Edition**
Staci Johnson and Rob Jenkins

Editorial Director: Joe Dougherty

Publisher, ESL and Dictionaries: Sherrise Roehr

Acquisitions Editor: Tom Jefferies

VP, Director of Content Development: Anita Raducanu

Development Editor: John Hicks

Director of Product Marketing: Amy T. Mabley

Executive Marketing Manager, U.S.: Jim McDonough

Senior Field Marketing Manager: Donna Lee Kennedy

Product Marketing Manager: Katie Kelley

Content Project Manager: Dawn Marie Elwell

Senior Print Buyer: Mary Beth Hennebury

Development Editor: Kasia McNabb

Development Editor: Catherine Mazur-Jefferies

Project Manager: Tunde Dewey

Composition: Pre-Press PMG

Cover and Interior Design: Studio Montage

Cover Art: ©Lisa Henderling/Getty Images

Illustrators: James Edwards; S.I. International

Photo Researcher: Erika Hokanson

Credits appear on page 177, which constitutes a continuation of the copyright page.

For product information and technology assistance, contact us at
Cengage Learning Customer & Sales Support, 1-800-354-9706
For permission to use material from this text or product,
submit all requests online at **www.cengage.com/permissions**
Further permissions questions can be emailed to
permissionrequest@cengage.com

Library of Congress Control Number: 2007905340

Student Edition

ISBN-13: 978-1-4240-0262-7

ISBN-10: 1-4240-0262-1

Heinle
20 Channel Center Street
Boston, MA 02210
USA

Cengage Learning is a leading provider of customized learning solutions with office locations around the globe, including Singapore, the United Kingdom, Australia, Mexico, Brazil, and Japan. Locate your local office at: **international.cengage.com/region**

Cengage Learning products are represented in Canada by Nelson Education, Ltd.

Visit Heinle online at **elt.heinle.com**

Visit our corporate website at **cengage.com**

Printed in Canada
3 4 5 6 7 11

ACKNOWLEDGMENTS

Elizabeth Aderman
New York City Board of Education, New York, NY

Sharon Baker
Roseville Adult School, Roseville, CA

Lillian Barredo
Stockton School for Adults, Stockton, CA

Linda Boice
Elk Grove Adult Education, Elk Grove, CA

Chan Bostwick
Los Angeles Unified School District, Los Angeles, CA

Debra Brooks
Manhattan BEGIN Program, New York, NY

Anne Byrnes
North Hollywood-Polytechnic Community Adult School, Sun Valley, CA

Rose Cantu
John Jay High School, San Antonio, TX

Toni Chapralis
Fremont School for Adults, Sacramento, CA

Melanie Chitwood
Miami-Dade College, Miami, FL

Geri Creamer
Stockton School for Adults, Stockton, CA

Stephanie Daubar
Harry W. Brewster Technical Center, Tampa, FL

Irene Dennis
San Antonio College, San Antonio, TX

Eileen Duffell
P.S. 64, New York, NY

Nancy Dunlap
Northside Independent School District, San Antonio, TX

Gloria Eriksson
Grant Skills Center, Sacramento, CA

Marti Estrin
Santa Rosa Junior College, Santa Rosa, CA

Lawrence Fish
Shorefront YM-YWHA English Language Program, Brooklyn, NY

Victoria Florit
Miami-Dade College, Miami, FL

Rhoda Gilbert
New York City Board of Education, New York, NY

Kathleen Jimenez
Miami-Dade College, Miami, FL

Nancy Jordan
John Jay High School Adult Education, San Antonio, TX

Renee Klosz
Lindsey Hopkins Technical Education Center, Miami, FL

David Lauter
Stockton School for Adults, Stockton, CA

Patricia Long
Old Marshall Adult Education Center, Sacramento, CA

Daniel Loos
Seattle Community College, Seattle, WA

Maria Miranda
Lindsey Hopkins Technical Education Center, Miami, FL

Karen Moore
Stockton School for Adults, Stockton, CA

George Myskiw
Malcolm X College, Chicago, IL

Heidi Perez
Lawrence Public Schools Adult Learning Center, Lawrence, MA

Marta Pitt
Lindsey Hopkins Technical Education Center, Miami, FL

Sylvia Rambach
Stockton School for Adults, Stockton, CA

Eric Rosenbaum
BEGIN Managed Programs, New York, NY

Laura Rowley
Old Marshall Adult Education Center, Sacramento, CA

Stephanie Schmitter
Mercer County Community College, Trenton, NJ

Amy Schneider
Pacoima Skills Center, Pacoima, CA

Sr. M. B. Theresa Spittle
Stockton School for Adults, Stockton, CA

Andre Sutton
Belmont Adult School, Los Angeles, CA

Jennifer Swoyer
Northside Independent School District, San Antonio, TX

Claire Valier
Palm Beach County School District, West Palm Beach, FL

Staci Johnson

Rob Jenkins

Ever since I can remember, I've been fascinated with other cultures and languages. I love to travel and every place I go, the first thing I want to do is meet the people, learn their language, and understand their culture. Becoming an ESL teacher was a perfect way to turn what I love to do into my profession. There's nothing more incredible than the exchange of teaching and learning from one another that goes on in an ESL classroom. And there's nothing more rewarding than helping a student succeed.

I love teaching. I love to see the expressions on my students' faces when the light goes on and their eyes show such sincere joy of learning. I knew the first time I stepped into an ESL classroom that this was where I needed to be and I have never questioned that resolution. I have worked in business, sales, and publishing, and I've found challenge in all, but nothing can compare to the satisfaction of reaching people in such a personal way.

We are so happy that instructors and agencies have embraced the lesson planning and project-based activities that we introduced in the first edition and are so enthusiastically teaching with **Stand Out**. It is fantastic that so many of our colleagues are as excited to be in this profession as we are. After writing over 500 lesson plans and implementing them in our own classrooms and after personal discussions with thousands of instructors all over the United States and in different parts of the world, we have found ourselves in a position to improve upon our successful model. One of the most notable things in the new edition is that we have continued to stress integrating skills in each lesson and have made this integration more apparent and obvious. To accomplish any life skill, students need to incorporate a combination of reading, writing, listening, speaking, grammar, pronunciation, and academic skills while developing vocabulary and these skills should be taught together in a lesson! We have accomplished this by extending the presentation of lessons in the book, so each lesson is more fully developed. You will also notice an extended list of ancillaries and a tighter correlation of these ancillaries to each book. The ancillaries allow you to extend practice on particular skill areas beyond the lesson in the text. We are so excited about this curriculum and know that as you implement it, you and your students will *stand out*.

Our goal is to give students challenging opportunities to be successful in their language-learning experience so they develop confidence and become independent, lifelong learners.

Staci Johnson
Rob Jenkins

ABOUT THE SERIES

The **Stand Out** series is designed to facilitate *active* learning while challenging students to build a nurturing and effective learning community.

The student books are divided into eight distinct units, mirroring competency areas most useful to newcomers. These areas are outlined in CASAS assessment programs and different state model standards for adults. Each unit in *Stand Out 4* is then divided into five lessons, a review, and a team project. Lessons are driven by performance objectives and are filled with challenging activities that progress from teacher-presented to student-centered tasks.

SUPPLEMENTAL MATERIALS

- The *Stand Out 4 Lesson Planner* is in full color with 60 complete lesson plans, taking the instructor through each stage of a lesson from warm-up and review through application.

- The *Stand Out 4 Activity Bank CD-ROM* has an abundance of customizable worksheets. Print or download and modify what you need for your particular class.

- The *Stand Out 4 Grammar Challenge* is a workbook that gives additional grammar explanation and practice in context.

- The *Reading and Writing Challenge* workbooks are designed to capture the principle ideas in the student book, and allow students to improve their vocabulary, academic, reading, and writing skills.

- The *Stand Out 4 Assessment CD-ROM with ExamView®* allows you to customize pre- and post-tests for each unit as well as a pre- and post-test for the book.

- Listening scripts are found in the back of the student book and the Lesson Planner. CDs are available with focused listening activities described in the Lesson Planner.

STAND OUT 4 LESSON PLANNER

The *Stand Out 4 Lesson Planner* is a new and innovative approach. As many seasoned teachers know, good lesson planning can make a substantial difference in the classroom. Students continue coming to class, understanding, applying, and remembering more of what they learn. They are more confident in their learning when good lesson planning techniques are incorporated.

We have developed lesson plans that are designed to be used each day and to reduce preparation time. The planner includes:

- Standard lesson progression (Warm-up and Review, Introduction, Presentation, Practice, Evaluation, and Application)

- A creative and complete way to approach varied class lengths so that each lesson will work within a class period.

- 180 hours of classroom activities

- Time suggestions for each activity

- Pedagogical comments

- Space for teacher notes and future planning

- Identification of LCP standards in addition to SCANS and CASAS standards

USER QUESTIONS ABOUT STAND OUT

- **What are SCANS and how do they integrate into the book?**
  SCANS is the Secretary's Commission on Achieving Necessary Skills. SCANS was developed to encourage students to prepare for the workplace. The standards developed through SCANS have been incorporated throughout the **Stand Out** student books and components.

  Stand Out addresses SCANS a little differently than do other books. SCANS standards elicit effective teaching strategies by incorporating essential skills such as critical thinking and group work. We have incorporated SCANS standards in every lesson, not isolating these standards in the work unit. All new texts have followed our lead.

- **What about CASAS?** The federal government has mandated that states show student outcomes as a prerequisite to receiving funding. Some states have incorporated the **C**omprehensive **A**dult **S**tudent **A**ssessment **S**ystem (CASAS) testing to standardize agency reporting. Unfortunately, many of our students are unfamiliar with standardized testing and therefore struggle with it. Adult schools need to develop lesson plans to address specific concerns. **Stand Out** was developed with careful attention to CASAS skill areas in most lessons and performance objectives.

- **Are the tasks too challenging for my students?**
  Students learn by doing and learn more when challenged. **Stand Out** provides tasks that encourage critical thinking in a variety of ways. The tasks in each lesson move from teacher-directed to student-centered so the learner clearly understands what's expected and is willing to "take a risk." The lessons are expected to be challenging. In this way, students learn that when they work together as a learning community, anything becomes possible. The satisfaction of accomplishing something both as an individual and as a member of a team results in greater confidence and effective learning.

- **Do I need to understand lesson planning to teach from the student book?** If you don't understand lesson planning when you start, you will when you finish! Teaching from **Stand Out** is like a course on lesson planning, especially if you use the Lesson Planner on a daily basis.

Stand Out does *stand out* because, when we developed this series, we first established performance objectives for each lesson. Then we designed lesson plans, followed by student book pages. The introduction to each lesson varies because different objectives demand different approaches. **Stand Out's** variety of tasks makes learning more interesting for the student.

- **What are team projects?** The final lesson of each unit is a **team project**. This is often a team simulation that incorporates the objectives of the unit and provides an additional opportunity for students to actively apply what they have learned. The project allows students to produce something that represents their progress in learning. These end-of-unit projects were created with a variety of learning styles and individual skills in mind. The team projects can be skipped or simplified, but we encourage instructors to implement them, enriching the overall student experience.

- **What do you mean by a customizable Activity Bank?** Every class, student, teacher, and approach is different. Since no one textbook can meet all these differences, the *Stand Out Activity Bank CD-ROM* allows you to customize **Stand Out** for your class. You can copy different activities and worksheets from the CD-ROM to your hard drive and then:

  - change items in supplemental vocabulary, grammar, and life skill activities;

  - personalize activities with student names and popular locations in your area;

  - extend every lesson with additional practice where you feel it is most needed.

The Activity Bank also includes the following resources:

- Multilevel worksheets – worksheets based on the standard worksheets described above but at one level higher and one level lower.

- Graphic organizer templates – templates that can be used to facilitate learning. They include graphs, charts, VENN diagrams, etc.

- Computer Worksheets – worksheets designed to supplement each unit and progress from simple to complex operations in word processing and spreadsheets for labs and computer enhanced classrooms.

- Internet Worksheets – worksheets designed to supplement each unit and provide application opportunities beyond the lessons in the book.

- **Is *Stand Out* grammar-based or competency-based?** **Stand Out** is a competency-based series; however, students are exposed to basic grammar structures. We believe that grammar instruction in context is extremely important. Grammar is a necessary component for achieving most competencies; therefore it is integrated into most lessons. Students are first provided with context that incorporates the grammar, followed by an explanation and practice. At this level, we expect students to learn basic structures but we do not expect them to acquire them. It has been our experience that students are exposed several times within their learning experience to language structures before they actually acquire them. For teachers who want to enhance grammar instruction, the *Activity Bank CD-ROM* and/or the *Grammar Challenge* workbooks provide ample opportunities.

The six competencies that drive **Stand Out** are basic communication, consumer economics, community resources, health, occupational knowledge, and lifelong learning (government and law replace lifelong learning in Books 3 and 4).

- **Are there enough activities so I don't have to supplement?** **Stand Out** stands alone in providing 180 hours of instruction and activities, even without the additional suggestions in the Lesson Planner. The Lesson Planner also shows you how to streamline lessons to provide 90 hours of classwork and still have thorough lessons if you meet less often. When supplementing with the *Stand Out Activity Bank CD-ROM*, the *Assessment CD-ROM with ExamView®*, and the *Stand Out Grammar Challenge* workbook, you gain unlimited opportunities to extend class hours and provide activities related directly to each lesson objective. Calculate how many hours your class meets in a semester and look to **Stand Out** to address the full class experience.

Stand Out is a comprehensive approach to adult language learning, meeting needs of students and instructors completely and effectively.

CONTENTS

• Grammar points that are explicitly taught   ◊ Grammar points that are presented in context   △ Grammar points that are being recycled

	Numeracy/ Academic Skills	EFF	SCANS	CASAS
Pre-Unit	• Writing a paragraph • Comparing and contrasting • Setting goals • Using a bar graph	Most EFF skills are incorporated into this unit with an emphasis on: • Taking responsibility for learning • Reflecting and evaluating • Conveying ideas in writing (Technology is optional.)	Many SCAN and EFF skills are incorporated in this unit with an emphasis on: • Understanding systems • Decision making	**1:** 0.1.2; 0.1.4; 0.2.1; 0.2.2 **2:** 0.2.1; 7.2.6 **3:** 0.1.2, 0.1.6, 0.2.1, 7.1.1
Unit 1	• Active reading • Focused listening • Writing a paragraph • Brainstorming • Using context clues • Using an outline • Comparing and contrasting • Reviewing	Most EFF skills are incorporated into this unit with an emphasis on: • Taking responsibility for learning • Reflecting and evaluating • Solving problems and making decisions • Planning (Technology is optional.)	Many SCAN and EFF skills are incorporated in this unit with an emphasis on: • Allocating time • Understanding systems • Applying technology to task • Responsibility • Self management • Writing • Decision making	**1:** 0.1.2, 0.2.4 **2:** 7.1.1, 7.1.2, 7.1.3, 7.2.5, 7.2.6 **3:** 7.1.1, 7.1.2, 7.1.3, 7.2.5, 7.2.6 **4:** 0.1.5, 7.4.1, 7.4.3, 7.4.5 **5:** 7.4.2 **R:** 7.2.1 **TP:** 4.8.1., 4.8.5., 4.8.6.
Unit 2	• Comparing and contrasting • Writing a business letter • Active reading • Focused listening • Calculating budgets • Reviewing	Most EFF skills are incorporated into this unit with an emphasis on: • Learning through research • Using mathematics in problem solving and communication • Planning (Technology is optional.)	Many SCAN skills are incorporated in this unit with an emphasis on: • Responsibility • Participating as a member of a team • Acquiring and evaluating information • Organizing and maintaining information • Decision making	

Contents

CONTENTS

• Grammar points that are explicitly taught   ◊ Grammar points that are presented in context   △ Grammar points that are being recycled

	Numeracy/ Academic Skills	EFF	SCANS	CASAS
Unit 3	• Pronunciation: Rising and Falling intonation • Active reading • Focused listening • Reading a bar graph • Sequencing • Writing about preferences • Summarizing a process • Comparing and contrasting • Using context clues • Reviewing	Most EFF skills are incorporated into this unit with an emphasis on: • Learning through research • Listening actively • Reading with understanding • Solving problems and making decisions • Planning (Technology is optional.)	Many SCAN skills are incorporated in this unit with an emphasis on: • Allocating money • Understanding systems • Monitoring and correcting performance • Interpreting and communicating information • Reading • Writing • Decision making	**1:** 1.4.1, 1.4.2 **2:** 1.4.2, 7.2.7 **3:** 1.4.4, 1.5.3 **4:** 1.5.1, 6.0.3, 6.0I.5, 6.1.1, 6.1.2 **5:** 1.4.7 **R:** 7.2.1 **TP:** 4.8.1, 4.8.5, 4.8.6.
Unit 4	• Pronunciation: Annunciation and Intonation • Focused listening • Making inferences • Reviewing	Most EFF skills are incorporated into this unit with an emphasis on: • Learning through research • Speaking so others can understand • Listening actively • Guiding others • Cooperating with others (Technology is optional.)	Many SCAN skills are incorporated in this unit with an emphasis on: • Understanding systems • Interpreting and communicating information • Writing • Decision making • Seeing things in the mind's eye	**1:** 0.1.2 **2:** 1.8.5, 2.5.6 **3:** 2.2.1, 2.2.5 **4:** 7.2.6 **5:** 7.2.2 **R:** 7.2.1 **TP:** 4.8.1, 4.8.5, 4.8.6
Unit 5	• Focused listening • Active reading • Using a bar graph • Calculating percentages • Skimming • Reviewing	Most EFF skills are incorporated into this unit with an emphasis on: • Learning through research • Reading with understanding • Using mathematics in problem solving and communication • Advocating and influencing (Technology is optional.)	Many SCAN skills are incorporated in this unit with an emphasis on: • Understanding systems • Self management • Acquiring and evaluating information • Interpreting and communicating information	**1:** 3.1.1, 3.1.3, 3.2.1 **2:** 3.1.1 **3:** 3.4.2, 3.5.9 **4:** 3.5.1, 3.5.3, 3.5.5 3.5.9, 6.7.3 **5:** 3.5.9 **R:** 7.2.1 **TP:** 4.8.1, 4.8.5, 4.8.6.

Contents

CONTENTS

● Grammar points that are explicitly taught   ◊ Grammar points that are presented in context   △ Grammar points that are being recycled

	Numeracy/ Academic Skills	EFF	SCANS	CASAS
Unit 6	• Active reading • Focused listening • Writing a resume • Writing a cover letter • Reviewing	Most EFF skills are incorporated into this unit, with an emphasis on: • Taking responsibility for learning • Conveying ideas in writing • Speaking so others can understand • Observing critically • Planning • Cooperating with others (Technology is optional.)	Most SCAN skills are incorporated in this unit with an emphasis on: • Self-esteem • Sociability • Acquiring and evaluating information • Speaking • Decision making	**1:** 4.1.8 **2:** 4.1.9 **3:** 4.1.3 **4:** 4.1.2 **5:** 4.1.5, 4.1.7 **R:** 7.2.1 **TP:** 4.8.1, 4.8.5, 4.8.6.
Unit 7	• Focused listening • Active reading • Reading a flowchart • Writing a description of a situation • Reviewing	Most EFF skills are incorporated into this unit with an emphasis on: • Speaking so others can understand • Listening actively • Observing critically • Solving problems and making decisions • Resolving conflict and negotiating • Cooperating with others (Technology is optional.)	Most SCAN skills are incorporated in this unit with an emphasis on: • Understanding systems • Participating as a member of a team • Acquiring and evaluating information	**1:** 4.1.9, 4.4.1 **2:** 4.2.1, 4.4.3 **3:** 4.2.1 **4:** 4.3.3, 4.3.4, 4.5.1 **5:** 4.4.1, 4.6.1 **R:** 7.2.1 **TP:** 4.8.1, 4.8.5, 4.8.6
Unit 8	• Focused listening • Active reading • Writing a paragraph • Writing a speech • Reading a flowchart • Writing a letter to a local official • Reviewing	Most EFF skills are incorporated into this unit with an emphasis on: • Taking responsibility for learning • Learning through research • Solving problems and making decisions (Technology is optional.)	Most SCAN skills are incorporated in this unit with an emphasis on: • Listening • Speaking • Responsibility • Self-esteem	1: 5.1.6 2: 5.1.4, 5.1.6 3: 5.1.4, 5.2.1 4: 5.5.7, 5.5.8 5: 5.1.6 R: 7.2.1 TP: 4.8.1, 4.8.5, 4.8.6.

Welcome to Stand Out, Second Edition

Stand Out works.

And now it works even better!

Built from the standards necessary for adult English learners, the second edition of *Stand Out* gives students the foundation and tools they need to develop confidence and become independent, lifelong learners.

- **Grammar** Charts clearly explain grammar points, and are followed by personalized exercises.
- Clear **grammar** explanations are followed by immediate practice, with a variety of activity types

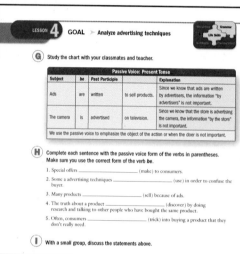

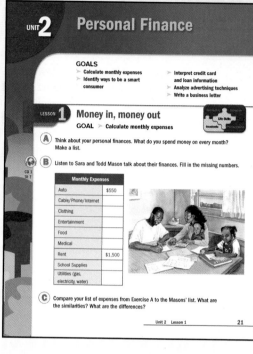

- Clearly defined **goals** provide a roadmap of learning for the student.
- State and federally required **life skills and competencies** are taught, helping students meet necessary benchmarks.

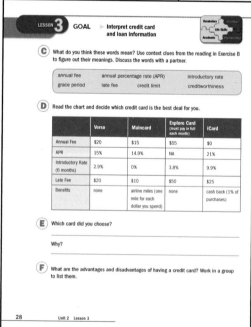

- A variety of **examples from real life**, like bank checks, newspaper ads, money, etc. help students learn to access the information and resources in their community.

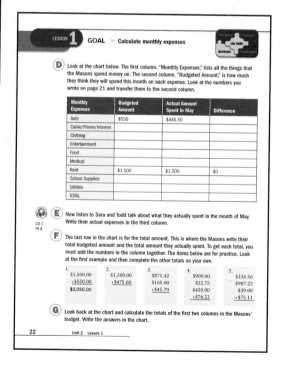

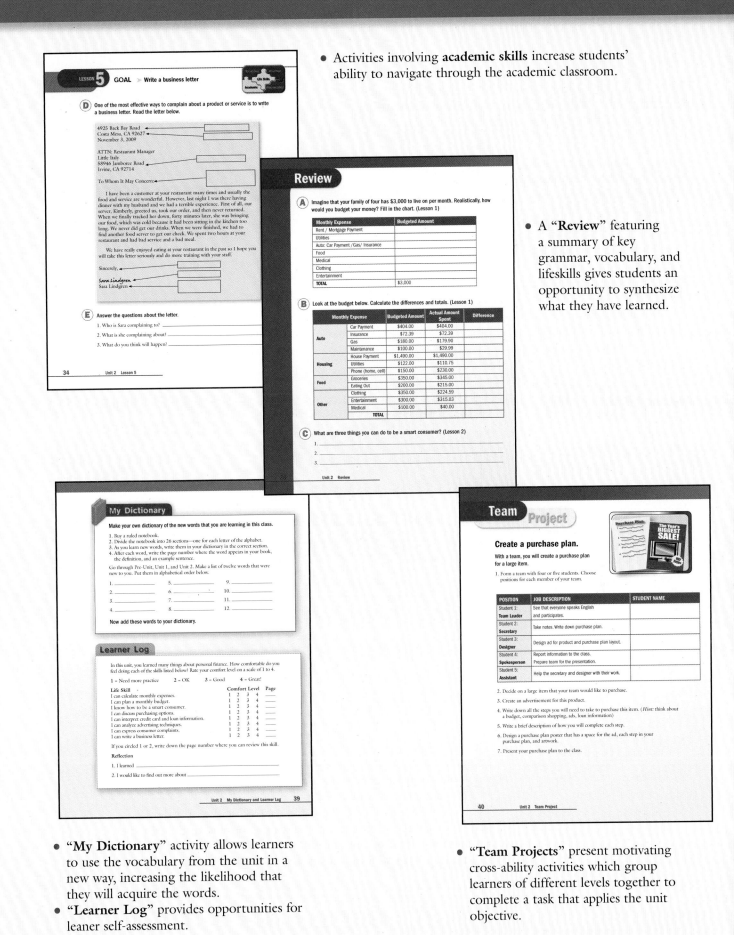

- Activities involving **academic skills** increase students' ability to navigate through the academic classroom.

- A **"Review"** featuring a summary of key grammar, vocabulary, and lifeskills gives students an opportunity to synthesize what they have learned.

- **"My Dictionary"** activity allows learners to use the vocabulary from the unit in a new way, increasing the likelihood that they will acquire the words.
- **"Learner Log"** provides opportunities for leaner self-assessment.

- **"Team Projects"** present motivating cross-ability activities which group learners of different levels together to complete a task that applies the unit objective.

The ground-breaking *Stand Out* Lesson Planners take the guesswork out of meeting the standards while offering high-interest, meaningful language activities, and three levels of pacing for each book.

- An at-a-glance **agenda** and **prep section** for each lesson ensure that instructors have a clear knowledge of what will be covered in the lesson.

- A complete **lesson plan** for each page in the student book is provided, following a standard lesson progression (Warm-up and Review, Introduction, Presentation, Practice, Evaluation, and Application).

- Clear, easy to identify **pacing guide** icons offer three different pacing strategies.

- **"Teaching Tips"** provide ideas and strategies for the classroom.

- **"Standards Correlations"** appear directly on the page, detailing how *Stand Out* meets CASAS, SCANS, and EFF standards.

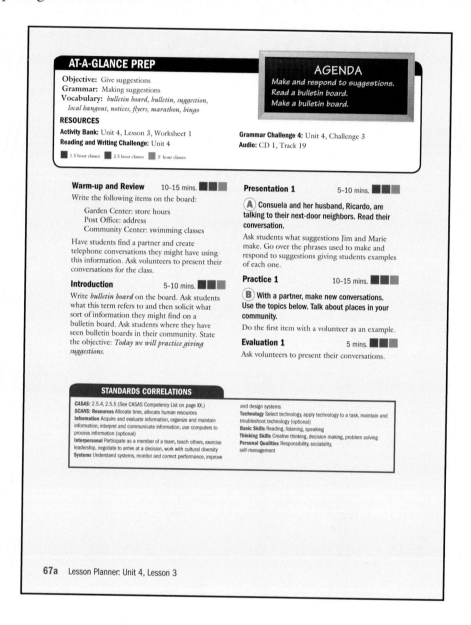

AT-A-GLANCE PREP

Objective: Give suggestions
Grammar: Making suggestions
Vocabulary: *bulletin board, bulletin, suggestion, local hangout, notices, flyers, marathon, bingo*

RESOURCES

Activity Bank: Unit 4, Lesson 3, Worksheet 1
Reading and Writing Challenge: Unit 4

Grammar Challenge 4: Unit 4, Challenge 3
Audio: CD 1, Track 19

■ 1.5 hour classes   ■ 2.5 hour classes   ■ 3⁺ hour classes

AGENDA

Make and respond to suggestions.
Read a bulletin board.
Make a bulletin board.

Warm-up and Review   10–15 mins. ■■■
Write the following items on the board:

  Garden Center: store hours
  Post Office: address
  Community Center: swimming classes

Have students find a partner and create telephone conversations they might have using this information. Ask volunteers to present their conversations for the class.

Introduction   5–10 mins. ■■■
Write *bulletin board* on the board. Ask students what this term refers to and then solicit what sort of information they might find on a bulletin board. Ask students where they have seen bulletin boards in their community. State the objective: *Today we will practice giving suggestions.*

Presentation 1   5–10 mins. ■■■
Ⓐ Consuela and her husband, Ricardo, are talking to their next-door neighbors. Read their conversation.
Ask students what suggestions Jim and Marie make. Go over the phrases used to make and respond to suggestions giving students examples of each one.

Practice 1   10–15 mins. ■■■
Ⓑ With a partner, make new conversations. Use the topics below. Talk about places in your community.
Do the first item with a volunteer as an example.

Evaluation 1   5 mins. ■■■
Ask volunteers to present their conversations.

STANDARDS CORRELATIONS

CASAS: 2.5.4, 2.5.5 (See CASAS Competency List on page XX.)
SCANS: **Resources** Allocate time, allocate human resources
Information Acquire and evaluate information, organize and maintain information, interpret and communicate information, use computers to process information (optional)
Interpersonal Participate as a member of a team, teach others, exercise leadership, negotiate to arrive at a decision, work with cultural diversity
Systems Understand systems, monitor and correct performance, improve and design systems
Technology Select technology, apply technology to a task, maintain and troubleshoot technology (optional)
Basic Skills Reading, listening, speaking
Thinking Skills Creative thinking, decision making, problem solving
Personal Qualities Responsibility, sociability, self-management

67a   Lesson Planner: Unit 4, Lesson 3

- Additional **supplemental activities** found on the *Activity Bank CD-ROM* are noted with an icon.
- The *Activity Bank CD-ROM* includes **reproducible multilevel activity masters** for each lesson that can be printed or downloaded and modified for classroom needs.
- **"Listening Scripts"** from the *Audio CD* are included.

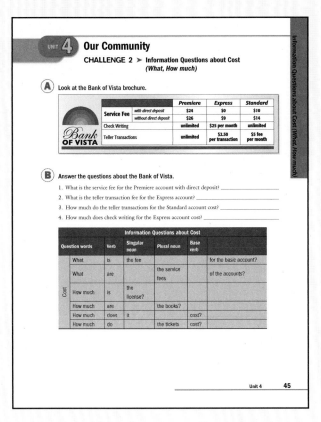

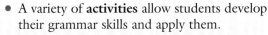

- *Grammar Challenge* workbooks include supplemental activities for students who desire even more contextual grammar and vocabulary practice.
- Clear and concise **grammar explanation boxes** provide a strong foundation for the activities.

The first sample page (Unit 4, page 45):

UNIT **4** **Our Community**

CHALLENGE 2 ➤ Information Questions about Cost
(*What, How much*)

Ⓐ Look at the Bank of Vista brochure.

		Premiere	Express	Standard
Service Fee	with direct deposit	$24	$0	$10
	without direct deposit	$26	$9	$14
Check Writing		unlimited	$25 per month	unlimited
Teller Transactions		unlimited	$2.50 per transaction	$5 fee per month

Bank OF VISTA

Ⓑ Answer the questions about the Bank of Vista.

1. What is the service fee for the Premiere account with direct deposit? _____
2. What is the teller transaction fee for the Express account? _____
3. How much do the teller transactions for the Standard account cost? _____
4. How much does check writing for the Express account cost? _____

Information Questions about Cost

	Question words	Verb	Singular noun	Plural noun	Base verb	
Cost	What	is	the fee			for the basic account?
	What	are		the service fees		of the accounts?
	How much	is	the license?			
	How much	are		the books?		
	How much	does	it		cost?	
	How much	do		the tickets	cost?	

Unit 4 **45**

The second sample page (Unit 4, page 46):

Ⓒ Complete each sentence with the correct form of *be* or *do*.

1. What _____are_____ the late fees for library books that are one week late?
2. What _____ the prices for different types of stamps?
3. How much _____ the bank charge for late fees?
4. What _____ the cost of a replacement ATM card?
5. How much _____ the textbooks for this class cost?
6. How much _____ the registration?
7. What _____ the fees for a new membership?
8. How much _____ the new mobile phones?
9. How much _____ each transaction?

Ⓓ Unscramble the words to make questions. Use the correct form of *be* or *do*.

1. be / what / late payments / for / the charges
   What are the charges for late payments?
2. be / what / for / new students / the / fees
   _____
3. much / school lunch / be / how / do / cost
   _____
4. library card/ what / a / be / of / price / the
   _____
5. boxes / be / how / for / much / mailing / the
   _____
6. do / copy cards / how / cost / much
   _____

Ⓔ Imagine you are going to open a new bank account. Write four questions you might ask about fees.

1. _____
2. _____
3. _____
4. _____

46 Unit 4

- A variety of **activities** allow students develop their grammar skills and apply them.
- Written by **Rob Jenkins** and **Staci Johnson**, the *Grammar Challenge* workbooks are directly aligned to the student books.

- *Reading & Writing Challenge* workbooks are also available. These workbooks provide challenging materials and exercises for students who want even more practice in reading, vocabulary development, and writing.

Getting to Know You

GOALS
➤ Fill out an admission application
➤ Identify learning strategies
➤ Write about your goals

LESSON 1

Tell me something about yourself.

GOAL ➤ Fill out an admission application

Vocabulary   Grammar
Life Skills
Academic   Pronunciation

A Imagine that you have decided to take classes at a college. Fill out the admission application below.

❧ CANYON COUNTY COLLEGE ❧
Admission Application

1. _____ _____ _____
        Last Name   *First Name*   *Middle Name*

2. Date of Birth ____/____/____ ____   3. _____-_____-_____   4. Place of Birth _____
              Mo   *Day*   *Year*   *Age*   *ID Number*   *City, State or Foreign Country*

5. Current address

   _____ _____ _____ _____
   Number and Street / Apt #   *City*   *State*   *Zip Code*

6. (____) ____-_____   7. _____
      (Area Code) Telephone Number   *Mother's Maiden Name*

8. Citizen of what country?

9. What is the highest level of education you have achieved?

10. What is your educational goal?

CD 1
TR 1

B Read the conversation. Then, listen to the conversation.

Bita: Hi. My name is Bita. What's your name?
Minh: I'm Minh. Nice to meet you.
Bita: Where are you from, Minh?
Minh: I'm from Vietnam. And you?
Bita: I'm from Iran.
Minh: Interesting. I've never been to Iran. Tell me something about yourself.
Bita: Well, I'm studying English because I want to be an architect in the United States.
Minh: Wow! That's ambitious. Good for you!
Bita: And tell me something about yourself, Minh.
Minh: In my free time, I make jewelry and sell it to help raise money for my grandchildren to go to college.
Bita: That's wonderful! I'd love to see your jewelry sometime.
Minh: I'd be more than happy to show it to you.

C Talk to three classmates. Find out their first names, where they are from, and one other piece of interesting information (a tidbit) about them. Then, introduce your new friends to another group of students.

First Name	Country	Interesting Tidbit

GOAL ➤ **Fill out an admission application**

D Find the first three students you talked to in Exercise C. Ask them questions about what they wrote on their applications on page P1. Use the questions below to help you get started.

What is your educational goal?
What is the highest level of education you have achieved?
Where were you born?
What is your mother's maiden name?

What are some other questions you might ask about their applications? Write two more questions below.

1. _____

2. _____

E Work with a group of four students. Write three questions you want to ask your classmates to help you get to know them.

1. _____

2. _____

3. _____

F Interview four *other* classmates and write their answers to your group's questions in the chart below. Go back to your group and share the information. At the end of this exercise, your group should have information about sixteen students!

Name	Question 1	Question 2	Question 3
1.			
2.			
3.			
4.			

Learning strategies

GOAL ➤ **Identify learning strategies**

A How do you learn English? Make a list.

1. Go to school.
2. _____
3. _____
4. _____
5. _____
6. _____

B Learning a new language takes place inside and outside the classroom. Below is a list of strategies you can use to learn a new language. Read them with your teacher.

Learning Strategies

Learn grammar rules.

Listen to the radio in English.

Read English books, magazines,

and newspapers.

Talk to native speakers.

Watch TV in English.

Write in English.

C Think of other learning strategies and add them to the list above.

D Answer the questions about your personal studying strategies.

1. Where do you usually study? _____

2. What strategies do you use inside the classroom? _____
_____

3. What strategies do you use outside the classroom? _____
_____

4. Write two strategies that you don't use now, but that you would like to use in the future. _____
_____

5. What do you think is the best strategy for learning English? _____
_____

E Interview other students in your class using the questions in Exercise D. Write their answers below. (If more than one student has the same answer, you don't need to write it twice.)

Study Locations	
Classroom Strategies	
Outside Strategies	
New Strategies to Use	
Best Strategies	

F Look at the bar graph and answer the questions.

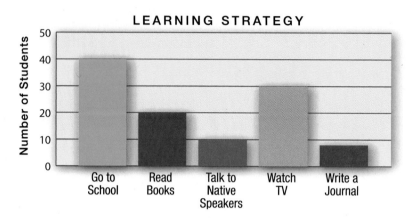

How many students. . .

go to school? _____

read books? _____

talk to native speakers? _____

watch TV? _____

keep a journal? _____

G With a group, decide on six effective learning strategies. Take a class poll to see how many people use these learning strategies.

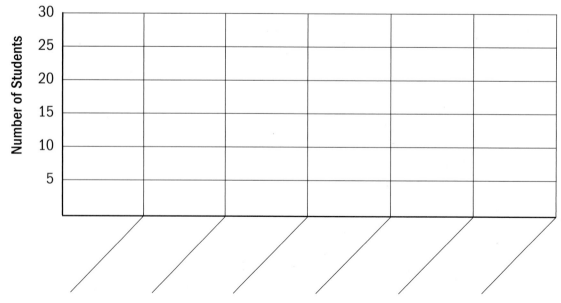

Our Class: Effective Learning Strategies

LESSON 3

What are your goals?

GOAL ➤ Write about your goals

A In this book, you will be learning many new strategies to help you learn and remember vocabulary. The first strategy involves word families. What do you think a word family is? Look at the example below.

Noun	Verb	Adjective	Adverb
creation	create	creative	creatively

B Read the paragraph. There are five words that belong to the same word family. Find and underline them.

> My goal for the year is to get organized. To learn a new language, you need to study a lot of vocabulary. Good organization requires writing down the new words you learn and finding out their meanings. You should organize the words in a notebook so you can easily find them. Once you learn how to keep a well-organized vocabulary list, you can say, "I have good organizational skills!"

C Complete the chart with word families. You may need to use a dictionary or ask another student for help.

Noun	Verb	Adjective	Adverb
		educational	
success			
	decide		
		achievable	XXXXX

D The student who wrote the paragraph in Exercise B has a goal—to get organized. What are your goals for the year? List them in the chart below.

My Goals

E Takuji has had three goals since he came to the United States. Read his paragraph. What are his three goals?

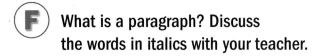

My Goals

   Ever since I came to the United States, I have had three goals. First, I want to improve my English by going to school every day and studying at night. Then, once my English is better, I will look for a job that pays more money. Finally, when I have saved up enough money, I will buy a new house for my family. These are the three goals that I made when I first came to the United States.

F What is a paragraph? Discuss the words in italics with your teacher.

   A paragraph is a group of sentences (usually 5–7 sentences) about the *same topic.* A *topic sentence* is usually the first sentence and it introduces your topic or *main idea. Support sentences* are the sentences that follow your topic sentence. They give *details* about your topic. A *conclusion sentence* is the last sentence of your paragraph and it summarizes what you have written.

G Look back at Takuji's paragraph. Can you find each of the three sentence types discussed in Exercise F?

H What are your goals? Write a paragraph about your goals on a piece of paper. Make sure your first sentence is a topic sentence. Follow your topic sentence with support sentences and then, finish your paragraph with a conclusion sentence.

GOAL ➤ Write about your goals

I Look at the first draft of Takuji's paragraph. There are eight errors. The first one has been done for you. Can you find and correct the rest?

My Goals

Ever since I came to the United States, I have had three goal. First I need
to improve my English by going at school every day and studying at night. Once my
English are better, I will look for a job that pays more money. Finally, when I have
saved up enough money. I will buy a house new for my family. This are the three goals
that I made when I first come to the united States.

J Write each of the errors from the paragraph in the chart below. Then, write the correct form and identify the type of error. Use choices from the box.

| punctuation | capitalization | subject/verb agreement | verb tense |
| spelling | singular/plural | word choice | word order |

Error	Correction	Type of Error
goal	goals	singular/plural

K Now exchange the paragraph you wrote in Exercise H with a partner. Check your partner's work for errors using the error types listed in Exercise J.

My Dictionary

Find three new words you learned in this unit. Write down the word and the sentence where you found the word.

EXAMPLE: Word: organizational   Page: P7
           Sentence: I have good organizational skills!

1. Word: _____   Page: _____

    Sentence: _____

2. Word: _____   Page: _____

    Sentence: _____

3. Word: _____   Page: _____

    Sentence: _____

Learner Log

In this unit, you had a chance to fill out an application, meet your classmates, identify learning strategies, and think about your goals. How comfortable do you feel doing each of the skills listed below? Rate your comfort level on a scale of 1 to 4.

1 = Need more practice   **2** = OK   **3** = Good   **4** = Great!

Life Skill	Comfort Level				Page
I can fill out an application form.	1	2	3	4	_____
I can tell others about myself.	1	2	3	4	_____
I can introduce my friends.	1	2	3	4	_____
I can identify learning strategies.	1	2	3	4	_____
I can create a bar graph.	1	2	3	4	_____
I can complete word families.	1	2	3	4	_____
I can write a paragraph.	1	2	3	4	_____
I can find and identify errors.	1	2	3	4	_____
I can edit a classmate's paragraph.	1	2	3	4	_____

If you circled a 1 or 2, write down the page number where you can review this skill.

Reflection

1. What was the most useful skill you learned in this unit? _____

2. How will this help you in life? _____

Balancing Your Life

GOALS

➤ Compare past and present
➤ Create a goal chart
➤ Identify obstacles and give advice

➤ Write about an important person
➤ Identify and apply time-management skills

Vocabulary · Grammar
Life Skills
Academic · Pronunciation

LESSON 1

Where did you use to study?

GOAL ➤ Compare past and present

CD 1
TR 2

A Bita and Minh are new students at Bellingham Adult School. Listen to their conversation on the first day of class.

B With a partner, answer the questions about Bita and Minh. You may have to guess some of the answers.

1. How old are they?
2. What do they do?
3. Where are they from?
4. Why are they studying English?

Minh

Bita

CD 1
TR 3

C Bita and Minh both talk about things they did in the past and things they do now. Listen again and complete the chart.

	Past	Now
Bita	went to another school in the daytime	
Minh		

GOAL ➤ **Compare past and present**

D Study the chart with your classmates and teacher.

Used to	
Example	**Rule**
Minh *used to* go to school during the day. Bita *used to* be an architect in Iran.	**Affirmative:** *used to* + base verb
Bita *did not use to* go to school at night. Minh *didn't use to* take care of his grandchildren.	**Negative:** *did* + *not (didn't)* + *use to* + base verb **Incorrect:** I didn't used to go to school.
Did Minh *use to* work? *Did* Bita *use to* study English?	**Yes/No Question:** *did* + subject + *use to* + base verb **Incorrect:** Did Bita used to live in Iran?
Where *did* Minh *use to* work? What *did* Bita *use to* study?	**Wh- Question:** *wh-* word + *did* + subject + *use to* + base verb
Used to + base verb expresses a past habit or state which is now different.	

E Complete the sentences with the correct form of *used to* and the base form of the verb in parentheses, or the simple present tense form of the verb.

EXAMPLE: Kaitlin ____used to live____ (live) with her family, but now she

____lives____ (live) alone.

1. Armando _____ (go) to school in the daytime, but now he

_____ (go) in the evening.

2. Where did Su _____ (teach)?

3. Heidi _____ (be) an administrative assistant now, but she

_____ (be) an architect in Sweden.

4. He _____ (go) to school and _____ (help) his

children now, but he _____ (assemble) computers.

5. Elisa _____ (live) near her family, but now she

_____ (live) far away.

6. Did the two brothers _____ (study) together?

F Look back at the things that you wrote about Bita and Minh in Exercise C. With a partner, make sentences about what Bita and Minh *used to* do and what they do now.

EXAMPLE: Bita used to go to another school in the daytime, but now she goes to school in the evening.

1. _____

2. _____

3. _____

G Write three *wh-* questions using *used to*. Then, ask a partner your questions.

EXAMPLE: Where did you used to work?

1. _____

2. _____

3. _____

H Look at the pictures. With a partner, make sentences comparing the past and the present.

Subject / Verb	Past	Present
1. Suzanne / play		
2. Eli and Rosa / live		

I Write two sentences comparing your past and present habits.

1. _____

2. _____

LESSON 2 Reaching your goals

GOAL ➤ **Create a goal chart**

 A Read the paragraph about Bita's goals. Use the context (surrounding words) to work out the meanings of the words in *italics*. Do the first one with your teacher.

My name is Bita and I'm from Iran. I've been in the United States for six years. In my country, I was an *architect* and I designed schools and hospitals, but in the United States, I don't have the right *qualifications* to be an architect. I have a plan. I'm going to learn English, go to school for architecture, and become an architect in the U.S. Here is my dream. In nine years, I will be an architect working in a *firm* with three other partners. We will design and build homes in *suburban* neighborhoods. I will live in a nice home that I designed, and I will look for the man of my dreams to share my life with. How does that sound to you?

 B Read the paragraph about Minh. Use the context to work out the meanings of the words in *italics*.

I'm Minh and I've been in the United States since 1975. I came here as a *refugee* from Vietnam. I used to work for a computer company, but now I'm *retired*. I help take care of my grandchildren while their parents are working, but I also do something else on the side. I make jewelry to sell to local jewelers. My father was a jeweler in Vietnam, and he taught me his art. My goal is to help send my grandchildren to college, so I save every penny I make from the jewelry. This is my dream. In five years, my oldest grandchild will teach elementary school in the community where she lives and she will *raise* her own family. My other grandchild will study medicine at one of the best schools in the country because he wants to be a *surgeon*. I hope that all of their dreams come true.

 C Answer the questions with a partner.

1. What are Bita's and Minh's goals?

2. What are they doing to make their goals a reality?

3. What are their dreams?

 D What are some examples of goals? Discuss your ideas with your teacher.

 E What are your future goals? Write them on a piece of paper.

GOAL ➤ **Create a goal chart**

CD 1
TR 4

F Listen to the conversation that Bita is having with her friend, Yoshiko. Fill in Bita's goal chart with the missing steps and dates.

Goal: To become an architect and a partner in a firm.	
Steps	Completion Dates
Step 1: Study English	Spring 2011
Step 2:	Fall 2011
Step 3:	
Step 4: Become an intern	Summer 2015
Step 5:	Winter 2016
Step 6: Become a partner in a firm	2017

G Turn back to page 4 and look at the paragraph about Minh. With a partner, create a goal chart for Minh based on the steps you think it will take Minh to achieve his goal.

Goal: For my granddaughter to be a teacher and my grandson to be a surgeon.	
Steps	Completion Dates
Step 1:	
Step 2:	
Step 3:	
Step 4:	
Step 5: My granddaughter will be a teacher and my grandson will be a surgeon.	

H Share your ideas with another pair of students.

I Look back at the goals you wrote in Exercise E. Choose the most important goal and write it below.

My goal: _____

By what year do you want to achieve your goal? _____

J Look at the goal chart below. Write your goal at the top. Write your goal again next to "Step 6," and write the date you will complete this goal. Now fill in the chart with the steps it will take to reach this goal. Estimate your completion dates.

Goal:	
Steps	**Completion Dates**
Step 1:	
Step 2:	
Step 3:	
Step 4:	
Step 5:	
Step 6:	

K Now talk to a partner about your goal and the steps that you will take to achieve it.

EXAMPLE: In the fall of 2010, I will take classes at a community college.

Future Tense Using *Will*	
Example	**Rule**
In the spring of 2009, *I will ask* my boss for a raise. In the summer, *I will look* for a job.	Future tense = *will* + base verb
In spoken English, people often use contractions: I will = *I'll*.	

 LESSON **3**

What should I do?

GOAL ➤ **Identify obstacles and give advice**

A Sometimes we have problems achieving our goals. These problems are called *obstacles*. In order to overcome these obstacles, it can be a good idea to brainstorm different possible solutions. Look at the diagram below.

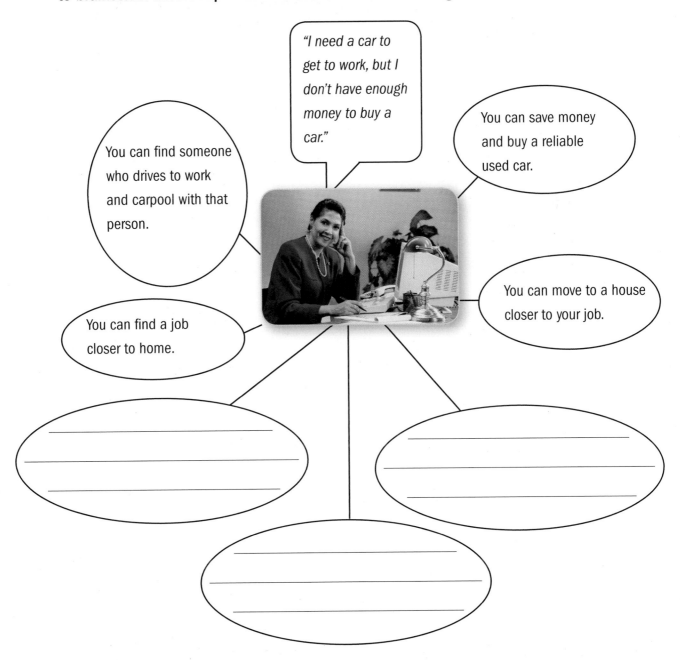

"*I need a car to get to work, but I don't have enough money to buy a car.*"

You can save money and buy a reliable used car.

You can find someone who drives to work and carpool with that person.

You can move to a house closer to your job.

You can find a job closer to home.

B Can you think of any other solutions? Add them to the blank circles in the cluster diagram above.

CD 1
TR 5

C Listen to each person talk to his or her friends about their problems. After you listen to each conversation, write the problem and two pieces of advice that the person receives.

Miyuki	Problem	Advice #1	Advice #2
Ron			
Patty			

D Read the ways of giving and responding to advice in the chart below.

Problem	Advice
Magda wants to go back to school, but she has two children that she has to take care of. One of them is a toddler who isn't in school yet.	*Why don't **you** ask your mother to take care of him?
	How about going to school in the evening?
	You should take some courses at home on the Internet.
	You could find a school with a daycare facility.

Response to advice (positive)	Response to advice (negative)
That's a great idea!	I don't think I can do that because . . .
Why didn't I think of that?	That doesn't sound possible because . . .
That's what I'll do.	That won't work because . . .

GOAL ➤ **Identify obstacles and give advice**

 Read the situations and come up with two possible solutions for each. Use *could* when writing your solutions.

EXAMPLE: Magda wants to go back to school, but she has two children that she has to take care of. One of her children is a toddler who isn't in school yet.

Solution: She could ask a family member to take care of her toddler so she can go to school during the day.

1. Frank wants to open up a restaurant in his neighborhood. He can get a loan to buy the property, but he won't have enough money to pay his employees until the restaurant starts making money.

Solution 1: _____

_____

Solution 2: _____

_____

2. Sergei works for a computer software company and wants to be promoted to project manager. The problem is that he needs to get more training before he can move up, but he doesn't have time to do training during the day.

Solution 1: _____

_____

Solution 2: _____

_____

 Work with a partner. Imagine that one of you has one of the problems in Exercise E. Make a conversation like the one below. Use different ways of giving and responding to advice.

EXAMPLE: *Student A:* I want to go back to school, but I have a young child to take care of.
Student B: Why don't you ask your mother to take care of him?
Student A: That won't work because she lives too far away.
Student B: Then how about taking some courses on the Internet?
Student A: That's a good idea!

G Look back at Exercise J on page 6. Think of an obstacle that might get in your way of achieving this goal. Make a cluster diagram like the one on page 7 and brainstorm different solutions with a partner.

What is most important to me?

GOAL ➤ Write about an important person

CD 1
TR 6

A Look at the photos and listen to Eliana talk about why they are important to her. Then, read the paragraphs.

This is a picture of the house where I grew up in Argentina. It's very important to me because it holds a lot of memories. This is the garden where I played with my brothers and sisters, and the veranda where I often sat with my parents in the evenings, listening to their stories and watching the stars and dreaming about my future.

This is the person who influenced me the most when I was young. She was my teacher in the first grade and we stayed friends until I left home. She was always so calm and gave me good advice. She was the kind of person who is able to give you another perspective on a problem and make you feel hopeful, no matter how troubled you are.

This is my daily journal. I use it to write about my feelings and hopes. It helps me understand them better. Sometimes I just write about things which happened to me during the day. My journal is something which helps me focus on the important things in my life.

B Read the paragraphs again and underline the words *who, which,* and *where.* When do we use these words? Circle the correct answers below.

1. We use (*which / where / who*) for places.
2. We use (*which / where / who*) for people.
3. We use (*which / where / who*) for things.

 C Study the chart with your teacher.

Adjective Clauses		
Main clause (Subject clause)	**Relative pronoun**	**Adjective clause**
This is the place	where	I grew up.
She is the person	who (that)	influenced me most.
A journal is something	which (that)	can help you focus on important things.
Main clause (Object clause)	**Relative pronoun**	**Adjective clause**
This is the woman	who (whom)	I met yesterday.
Here is the book	which	you gave me this morning.
Adjectival clauses describe a preceding noun. They can describe a subject noun or an object noun. If the noun is an object, you can leave out the relative pronoun.		

D Combine the sentences using adjective clauses. In which sentence can you leave out the relative pronoun?

EXAMPLE: This is the house. I grew up there.

<u>This is the house where I grew up.</u>

1. That is the city. I was born there.

_____

2. I have a friend. She helps me when I am sick.

_____

3. We have some neighbors. They are very friendly.

_____

4. This is the gold ring. My mother bought it for me.

_____

 E Look at the pictures with a partner, and make sentences about them using adjective clauses.

GOAL ➤ **Write about an important person**

F Bita wrote a paragraph about her brother. Read the paragraph. With a partner, discuss the questions that follow.

Someone Who Has Influenced Me

The person who has influenced me most in my life is my brother, Karim. I admire my brother for three reasons. First, he has patience and determination. Second, he does a fantastic job helping the community. Third, he is the type of person who always has time for his friends and family, no matter how busy he is. He has had a very positive influence on my life.

1. What type of person is Bita's brother?
2. Why does Bita admire him?
3. How has he influenced Bita?

G Now it's your turn to write about a person who has influenced you. Complete these pre-writing activities before you begin.

➤ **Brainstorm** (Think about your ideas before you write.)

Who has influenced you most in your life? _____

Why is this person so important to you? List three reasons.

1. _____
2. _____
3. _____

➤ **Introduce** (Tell your readers what you are writing about.) Write your topic sentence.

_____

➤ **Conclude** (Remind your reader of the main idea, but don't restate your topic sentence.) Write your conclusion sentence.

_____

H Now write a paragraph about an important person in your life. Start with your topic sentence. Put your reasons (support sentences) in the middle of your paragraph and finish with your conclusion sentence.

Time management

GOAL ➤ Identify and apply time-management skills

 A Are you an organized person? Do you . . .

- ❑ try to do everything but run out of time?
- ❑ always plan everything far in advance?
- ❑ dislike planning things too far ahead?
- ❑ tend to leave things to the last minute?
- ❑ get upset by last-minute changes to your schedule?
- ❑ only plan for important tasks like exams and job interviews?

Important	Very Important	URGENT!

 B Work with a partner to list time-management strategies that you know.

Time-Management Strategies

1. keep a schedule

C Talk to other pairs in your class. What are some strategies they came up with that are not on your list? Write them below.

More Time-Management Strategies

GOAL ➤ Identify and apply
time-management skills

D Read the paragraphs about time management. Write the number
of the corresponding paragraph next to each topic below.

____ How can I get everything done?

____ Why is good health important to time management?

____ How can I be organized?

____ How can I manage my time? Why is it important?

____ How can I get important tasks done first?

Time-Management Skills

(1) Finding enough time to study is very important for all students. There are a number of time-management strategies that can help you to manage your time wisely. You can use them to *accomplish* the goals you have set for yourself without *sacrificing* the time you spend with your family and friends.

(2) One of the best ways to stay organized is to keep a schedule. First, write down everything you need to do in a week. This includes work, study, taking care of children, shopping, and other tasks. Next, *allocate* a time slot to complete each of these tasks. Be *realistic* about the time you will need for each task. Mark these *deadlines* on your schedule. Finally, check off each task when you have completed it.

(3) It is a good idea to *prioritize* your tasks in order of importance. First, make a "To Do" list of all your tasks. Second, divide your list into three groups: A, B, and C. The A list is for tasks you need to do today. The B list is for tasks you need to do tomorrow. The C list is for tasks you need to do sometime this week. Dividing your list will help you get your most important tasks done first. You can also list tasks according to urgency: tasks you have to do, tasks you should do, and tasks you'd like to do if you have time.

(4) Another time-management strategy is to combine two or more tasks and do them *simultaneously*. You can listen to audio study tapes while you are driving, for example. Or, you can review verb tenses while you are eating lunch.

(5) Lastly, remember that good health is also important to managing your time effectively. If you are burned out or overtired, you cannot do your best. First, you need to allow time for rest and exercise. Also, you need to have time to spend with family, friends, and people who are important to you.

In conclusion, don't get upset if you cannot accomplish all your goals. Be positive about your *achievements* and reward yourself for goals that you have accomplished.

E Find the following words in the reading and use the context to work out their meanings:
accomplish, sacrificing, allocate, realistic, deadlines, prioritize, simultaneously, achievements.

F Use the diagram below to record the main points of the reading.

Time-Management Strategies	Keep a schedule.	Write down everything you need to do in a week.
		Allocate a time slot to complete each task.
		Check off each task when completed.
	Combine two or more tasks.	

G Think about what you learned today and complete the chart.

My Time-Management Strategies	
Strategies I Use Now	**New Strategies I Will Start Using**

Review

A Make sentences to contrast past and present habits. (Lesson 1)

EXAMPLE:

Past: I ate meat.   Present: I don't eat meat now.

I used to eat meat, but now I don't.

1. Past: Paolo didn't have a computer.   Present: He has a computer.

_____

2. Past: Maria swam every day.   Present: She doesn't swim now.

_____

3. Past: My children didn't like vegetables.   Present: They like vegetables now.

_____

4. Past: I didn't study full time.   Present: Now I study full time.

_____

B Write four questions using the correct form of *used to* that you can ask your partner. Leave the answer lines blank for now. (Lesson 1)

EXAMPLE: Where did you used to live? _____

ANSWER: _____

1. _____

Answer: _____

2. _____

Answer: _____

3. _____

Answer: _____

4. _____

Answer: _____

Now ask your partner the questions and write down his or her answers.

C Ask a partner about one of his or her goals and complete a goal chart with the information he or she gives you. (Lesson 2)

Goal: _____	
Steps	Completion Dates
Step 1:	
Step 2:	
Step 3:	
Step 4:	

D Dave wants to study at college, but he needs to work full time while he is going to school in order to pay for his education and support his family. Dave asks his friend, Camille, for advice. With a partner, create a conversation between the two friends. Make sure Camille suggests two or three different solutions to Dave's problem. Use expressions from this unit for giving and responding to advice. (Lesson 3)

Dave: _____

Camille: _____

Dave: _____

Camille: _____

Dave: _____

Camille: _____

Dave: _____

E Combine the sentences using adjective clauses. (Lesson 4)

1. Esra has many brothers and sisters. They live in Argentina.

   _____

2. This is a good grammar book. It can help you improve your writing.

   _____

3. I am trying to find a school. I can study computers.

   _____

4. E-mail is a type of communication. We use it at home and at work.

   _____

Review

(Lesson 5)

F Read the list of statements below. Write *TM* next to the ones that are time-management strategies. (Lesson 5)

___ Become an architect.

___ Buy new clothes.

___ Check off your tasks when you have finished them.

___ Combine two tasks.

___ Give advice.

___ Keep a schedule.

___ Make jewelry.

___ Prioritize your tasks.

___ Send your children to college.

___ Set realistic deadlines.

___ Stay healthy.

___ Write about your teacher.

G Use the words from the box to complete the sentences. (Lessons 1-5)

deadline	prioritize	simultaneously
raising	refugee	retired

1. Someone who stops work because they are old is _____.

2. Someone who escapes from a country because of danger is a

   _____.

3. If you have young children, you are _____ a family.

4. If you are doing two things at the same time, you are doing them

   _____.

5. If you have to complete a task by a certain time, that is your

   _____.

6. When you put things in order of importance, you _____ them.

My Dictionary

It is useful to make vocabulary cards to help you practice new vocabulary words and phrases. Look at the sample card below.

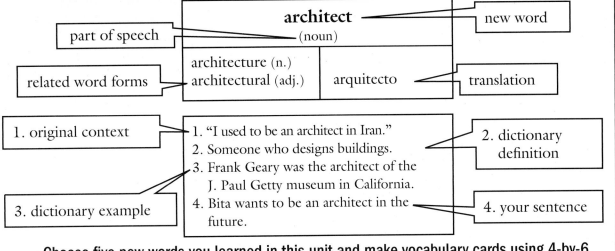

| part of speech | **architect** (noun) | | new word |
| related word forms | architecture (n.) architectural (adj.) | arquitecto | translation |

| 1. original context | 1. "I used to be an architect in Iran." 2. Someone who designs buildings. 3. Frank Geary was the architect of the J. Paul Getty museum in California. 4. Bita wants to be an architect in the future. | 2. dictionary definition |
| 3. dictionary example | | 4. your sentence |

Choose five new words you learned in this unit and make vocabulary cards using 4-by-6 index cards. If you don't have cards, use pieces of paper.

Learner Log

In this unit, you learned many things about balancing your life. How comfortable do you feel doing each of the skills listed below? Rate your comfort level on a scale of 1 to 4.

1 = Need more practice   **2** = OK   **3** = Good   **4** = Great!

Life Skill	Comfort Level				Page
I can compare the past and present.	1	2	3	4	_____
I can create a goal chart.	1	2	3	4	_____
I can identify obstacles and solutions.	1	2	3	4	_____
I can give and respond to advice.	1	2	3	4	_____
I can write about an important person.	1	2	3	4	_____
I can identify time-management skills.	1	2	3	4	_____
I can use context clues to discover word meaning.	1	2	3	4	_____
I can analyze time-management techniques.	1	2	3	4	_____

If you circled 1 or 2, write down the page number where you can review this skill.

Reflection

1. I learned _____.

2. I would like to find out more about _____.

3. I am still confused about _____.

Team Project

Create a goal chart.

With a team, you will create a goal chart for goals you want to accomplish in this class.

1. Form a team with four or five students. Choose positions for each member of your team.

GOAL CHART

STEPS	COMPLETION DATE
STEP 1:	
STEP 2:	
STEP 3:	
STEP 4:	
STEP 5:	
STEP 6:	

POSITION	JOB DESCRIPTION	STUDENT NAME
Student 1: **Team Leader**	See that everyone speaks English and participates.	
Student 2: **Secretary**	Take notes.	
Student 3: **Designer**	Design the goal chart.	
Student 4: **Spokesperson**	Prepare team for presentation.	
Student 5: **Assistant**	Help team members with their jobs.	

2. Decide on one goal that your team would like to accomplish by the end of this class. Make it specific. ("Learn English" is not a very specific goal, but "improve our reading skills" and "learn more vocabulary" are.)

3. Write down the steps it will take to reach this goal. Write down a completion date for each step.

4. Write down two obstacles that might get in the way of achieving your goal and possible solutions for each one.

5. Make a list of three time-management techniques that will help you reach your goal.

6. Design a goal chart that includes all of the information from Steps 2–5.

7. Present your chart to the class.

Personal Finance

GOALS

➤ Calculate monthly expenses
➤ Identify ways to be a smart consumer

➤ Interpret credit card and loan information
➤ Analyze advertising techniques
➤ Write a business letter

LESSON 1

Money in, money out

GOAL ➤ Calculate monthly expenses

A Think about your personal finances. What do you spend money on every month? Make a list.

CD 1
TR 7

B Listen to Sara and Todd Mason talk about their finances. Fill in the missing numbers.

Monthly Expenses	
Auto	$550
Cable/Phone/Internet	
Clothing	
Entertainment	
Food	
Medical	
Rent	$1,500
School Supplies	
Utilities (gas, electricity, water)	

C Compare your list of expenses from Exercise A to the Masons' list. What are the similarities? What are the differences?

D Look at the chart below. The first column, "Monthly Expenses," lists all the things that the Masons spend money on. The second column, "Budgeted Amount," is how much they think they will spend this month on each expense. Look at the numbers you wrote on page 21 and transfer them to the second column.

Monthly Expenses	Budgeted Amount	Actual Amount Spent in May	Difference
Auto	$550	$445.50	
Cable/Phone/Internet			
Clothing			
Entertainment			
Food			
Medical			
Rent	$1,500	$1,500	$0
School Supplies			
Utilities			
TOTAL			

E Now listen to Sara and Todd talk about what they actually spent in the month of May. Write their actual expenses in the third column.

CD 1
TR 8

F The last row in the chart is for the total amount. This is where the Masons write their total budgeted amount and the total amount they actually spent. To get each total, you must add the numbers in the column together. The items below are for practice. Look at the first example and then complete the other totals on your own.

1.
$1,500.00
+$550.00
$2,050.00

2.
$1,300.00
+$475.60

3.
$875.42
$165.00
+$45.70

4.
$900.00
$32.75
$450.00
+$76.22

5.
$234.56
$987.23
$39.00
+$75.11

G Look back at the chart and calculate the totals of the first two columns in the Masons' budget. Write the answers in the chart.

GOAL ➤ **Calculate monthly expenses**

H The last *column* of the chart is for the difference between the amount of money the Masons budgeted for each expense and what they actually spent. To make this calculation, you must use subtraction. The items below are for practice. Look at the first example and then complete the other differences on your own.

1.	2.	3.	4.	5.
$550.00	$1,300.00	$875.42	$450.00	$987.23
−$445.50	−$475.60	−$165.00	−$76.22	−$75.11
$104.50				

*Note: When doing subtraction, the larger number must be on top.

I Sometimes the Masons budgeted *less* than they spent. (For example, they spent more on utilities than they budgeted.) In this case, you still do the subtraction with the larger number on top, but the end result is a negative number.

The items below are for practice. Look at the first example and then complete the other differences on your own.

They budgeted:		$160.00	$85.00	$200.00
They spent:		$208.12	$100.10	$213.45
	1.	2.	3.	

1.	2.	3.
$208.12	$100.10	$213.45
−$160.00	−$85.00	−$200.00
$48.12		

J Calculate the differences between the first two columns in the Masons' budget. Write the answers in the chart.

K Make a budget of your own, estimating the amount of all of your expenses. Then, keep track of how much money you actually spend over the next month. Finally, calculate the difference between the amount you budgeted and the amount you actually spent.

Savvy shopper

GOAL ➤ **Identify ways to be a smart consumer**

 A The Masons have decided to buy a new couch for their home. They want a good-quality piece of furniture that will last a long time. What do you think they will do before buying the couch? Discuss your ideas with your classmates.

 B Sara did some research on the Internet. Read the web page below to see what information she found.

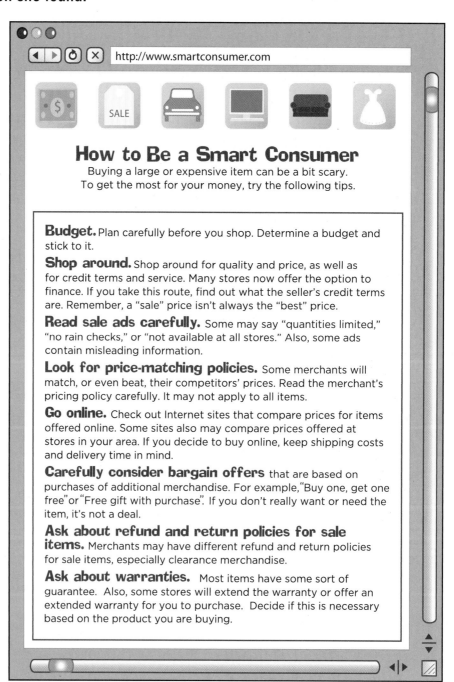

http://www.smartconsumer.com

How to Be a Smart Consumer
Buying a large or expensive item can be a bit scary.
To get the most for your money, try the following tips.

Budget. Plan carefully before you shop. Determine a budget and stick to it.

Shop around. Shop around for quality and price, as well as for credit terms and service. Many stores now offer the option to finance. If you take this route, find out what the seller's credit terms are. Remember, a "sale" price isn't always the "best" price.

Read sale ads carefully. Some may say "quantities limited," "no rain checks," or "not available at all stores." Also, some ads contain misleading information.

Look for price-matching policies. Some merchants will match, or even beat, their competitors' prices. Read the merchant's pricing policy carefully. It may not apply to all items.

Go online. Check out Internet sites that compare prices for items offered online. Some sites also may compare prices offered at stores in your area. If you decide to buy online, keep shipping costs and delivery time in mind.

Carefully consider bargain offers that are based on purchases of additional merchandise. For example, "Buy one, get one free" or "Free gift with purchase". If you don't really want or need the item, it's not a deal.

Ask about refund and return policies for sale items. Merchants may have different refund and return policies for sale items, especially clearance merchandise.

Ask about warranties. Most items have some sort of guarantee. Also, some stores will extend the warranty or offer an extended warranty for you to purchase. Decide if this is necessary based on the product you are buying.

LESSON 2

GOAL ➤ **Identify ways to be a smart consumer**

 C Based on the reading in Exercise B, list six things you should do before you make a large purchase.

1. _____
2. _____
3. _____
4. _____
5. _____
6. _____

 D Sometimes being a smart consumer means not buying something even when you want it. If you had all the money in the world, what two items would you buy?

1. _____   2. _____

Now look at these examples:
1. If I were rich, I would buy a new car. (I'm not really rich, so I can't buy a new car.)
2. If they had a million dollars, they would move to Beverly Hills. (They don't have a million dollars, so they can't move to Beverly Hills.)

These statements are called *contrary-to-fact conditionals*. They express a condition and a result that are not true at this point in time.

E Study the chart with your teacher.

Contrary-to-Fact Conditionals	
Condition (*if* + past tense verb)	**Result (*would* + base verb)**
If she *got* a raise,	she *would buy* a new house.
If they *didn't spend* so much money on rent,	they *would have* more money for entertainment.
If I *were* a millionaire,	I *would give* all my money to charity.
If John *weren't* so busy at work,	he *would spend* more time with his children.

- *Contrary-to-fact* (or *unreal*) *conditional statements* are sentences that are not true.
- The *if*-clause can come in the first or second part of the sentence. Notice how commas are used in the examples. (If you reverse the order of the condition and result clauses, omit the comma.)
- In written English, use *were* (instead of *was*) for *if*-clauses with first and third person singular forms of *be*.
- In spoken English, people often use contractions: I would = *I'd*; she would = *she'd*, etc.

F Complete the sentences with the correct form of the verbs in parentheses.

1. If Bita _____ (be) an architect in the United States, she _____ (design) beautiful homes.

2. Van's parents _____ (purchase) a new computer if they _____ (have) some extra money.

3. If my husband _____ (be) rich, he _____ (buy) me an expensive diamond ring.

4. George _____ (save) more money if he _____ (not spend) so much on eating out.

5. You _____ (not be) so tired if you _____ (have) more time to relax.

G Study the chart with your teacher.

Contrary-to-Fact Questions	
Wh-Question	**Yes/No Question**
What + *would* + subject + base verb + *if* + subject + past tense	*Would* + subject + base verb + *if* + subject + past tense
What would you do *if* you won the lottery?	*Would* you give up your job *if* you won the lottery?

H Work in groups. Take turns asking your group the questions below. Each person must answer with a conditional statement.

EXAMPLE: *Student A:* What would you do if you won the lottery?
Student B: If I won the lottery, I'd buy a house.
Student C: If I won the lottery, I'd travel around the world.

What would you do if . . .

1. you had a million dollars?
2. you lived in a mansion?
3. you had your own airplane?

4. you were the boss of a huge company?
5. you owned an island in the Pacific?
6. (your own idea)?

I Write three statements about what *you* would do if you won the lottery.

1. _____

2. _____

3. _____

Charge it!

GOAL ➤ Interpret credit card and loan information

A Do you have a credit card? What kind of card is it? What is the interest rate? What do you use it for? Discuss these questions with your group.

B Read the information below about credit cards.

What do I need to know before applying for a credit card?

What is a credit card and how is it different from a debit card? A credit card is a flexible way of borrowing money to make a purchase and paying back the money later. A debit card is a way of taking money directly from your bank account.

Annual fee: Many issuers charge an *annual* fee for using their card—typically between $15 and $50. If you do not plan to pay your bill within a month or two from the date you make a purchase, you should probably look for a card with no annual fee.

Annual percentage rate (APR): APR can be either "fixed" or "variable." Fixed rate APRs are usually a little higher, but you know exactly how much you will be charged each month.

Introductory rate: Some credit cards offer a low *introductory rate* that switches to a higher rate later. Make sure that you know how long the introductory rate is applicable and what APR the card will carry after the introductory period. Be aware that the introductory rate for some cards will be terminated if you are late with a payment.

Grace period: The *grace period* is the time between the day you make a purchase and the day when interest begins to be charged. For most cards, it is 25 days from the billing date. Many cards have no grace period and you will pay interest from the date you make a purchase.

Other fees: How much is the penalty for being late? How much do you pay if you go over the *credit limit*? How much does your bank charge you for an ATM withdrawal (cash advance fee)? Is the interest rate for cash advances the same or is it higher than the card's "regular" APR? What is your cash advance limit? Answers to all these questions may influence your choice of credit card.

Benefits: A number of issuers offer additional benefits to card members. Rebate cards allow you to earn cash back and discounts on goods and services based on card usage. Frequent flyer cards allow you to earn miles for each dollar charged.

How do issuers evaluate if I am creditworthy?
Issuers determine *creditworthiness* by what are called the three Cs of credit (capacity, collateral, and character). **Capacity** refers to your ability to pay based on your income and existing debt. **Collateral** refers to any assets you have that can secure payment (e.g., your savings or home ownership). **Character** refers to factors such as your payment history and length of employment. The criteria for accepting applicants vary between issuers and credit card products.

LESSON 3 **GOAL** ➤ **Interpret credit card and loan information**

C What do you think these words mean? Use context clues from the reading in Exercise B to figure out their meanings. Discuss the words with a partner.

annual fee	annual percentage rate (APR)	introductory rate
grace period	late fee	credit limit	creditworthiness

D Read the chart and decide which credit card is the best deal for you.

	Verso	Maincard	Explore Card (must pay in full each month)	iCard
Annual Fee	$20	$15	$55	$0
APR	15%	14.9%	NA	21%
Introductory Rate (6 months)	2.9%	0%	3.8%	9.9%
Late Fee	$20	$10	$50	$25
Benefits	none	airline miles (one mile for each dollar you spend)	none	cash back (1% of purchases)

E Which card did you choose?

_____

Why?

_____

F What are the advantages and disadvantages of having a credit card? Work in a group to list them.

LESSON **3** **GOAL** ➤ **Interpret credit card and loan information**

 G **Read the information about loans.**

When you decide to purchase something that costs more than you can pay right now, you can put it on your credit card or you can get a loan. A loan from a bank or lending institution is something you have to apply for. You usually have to specify the amount you want to borrow and what kind of purchase you want to make. For large purchases, you usually need collateral, such as your house, your business, or a down payment. The interest rate will vary according to the amount you borrow, where you borrow the money from, and your creditworthiness.

H **With a partner, discuss the differences between these purchasing options. Make notes in the chart.**

Loan	Credit Card

I **Look at the list of items. For each item, decide if you should get a loan or put it on a credit card. Discuss your answers with a group.**

	Car	College Course	TV	Computer	Airline Ticket	Small Business
loan						
credit card						

How they pull you in

GOAL ➤ Analyze advertising techniques

A Look at the ads for digital camcorders.

1 JUST ARRIVED!

SONIC
RS-200
MINIDV

30x optical zoom • 1000x digital zoom
2.5" LCD screen • built-in light
color viewfinder • image stabilization
$329 (with 20% off coupon)

2 ✧ **One-touch recording!** ✧

$399

Canyon
ZT500
miniDV

**25x optical zoom
1000x digital zoom
digital still mode
sleep button
2.7" LCD screen**

3 *Great for the professional!*

Tihachi
miniDVD

weighs *less than a pound!*

$799
(after $100 rebate)

★ digital still mode
★ 25x optical zoom
★ 1200x digital zoom
★ includes **FREE** camera bag

4 Perfect family camcorder!

$299

Niken
miniDV

20x optical zoom

2.5" LCD screen • digital still mode • includes extra battery

---

miniDV: records video to small cassette tapes

miniDVD: records video to small DVDs

optical zoom: uses the lens of the camera to bring the subject closer
without sacrificing quality

digital zoom: crops the image and then digitally enlarges it on your screen. This process
does sacrifice quality.

B Discuss these questions with a group.

1. Which ad is the most attractive to you? Why?
2. What kind of information do the ads give?
3. What information is not included?
4. How do the ads try to persuade you to buy the products?

C Look at the ads on page 30 to complete the chart. If the information is missing from the ad, write *doesn't say*.

	Sonic	Canyon	Tihachi	Niken
Price	$329			
Coupon or rebate needed?		no		
Digital zoom				doesn't say
Optical zoom		25x		
Digital still mode			yes	
LCD screen size	2.5″			
Recording media		miniDV		
Other		sleep button		
Special offers			free camera bag	

D Is there anything else that you would like to know about the camcorders? Write three questions that you might ask a salesperson.

1. _____

2. _____

3. _____

E Based on the advertisements, which camera would you buy?

F Discuss these questions with a group.

1. What do advertisers do to get you interested in their products?
2. Can you always trust advertisements?
3. What's the best way to find out the truth about a product?

G Study the chart with your classmates and teacher.

Passive Voice: Present Tense				
Subject	**Be**	**Past Participle**		**Explanation**
Ads	are	written	to sell products.	Since we know that ads are written by advertisers, the information "by advertisers" is not important.
The camera	is	advertised	on television.	Since we know that the store is advertising the camera, the information "by the store" is not important.
We use the passive voice to emphasize the object of the action or when the doer is not important.				

H Complete each sentence with the passive voice form of the verbs in parentheses. Make sure you use the correct form of the verb **be**.

1. Special offers _____ (make) to consumers.

2. Some a advertising techniques _____ (use) in order to confuse the buyer.

3. Many products _____ (sell) because of ads.

4. The truth about a product _____ (discover) by doing research and talking to other people who have bought the same product.

5. Often, consumers _____ (trick) into buying a product that they don't really need.

I With a small group, discuss the statements above.

J Imagine that you and a group of students are part of an advertising firm. Choose a product to write an ad for. Try to persuade people to buy your product. Use some passive voice sentences in your ad! Share your ad with the class.

Express yourself

GOAL ➤ Write a business letter

A Tell your classmates about a time when you complained about a product or service.

B Read each situation below. Answer the questions with a partner.

1. You got home from the grocery store and realized the milk is sour. Who would you talk to? <u>the grocery store manager</u>

   What would you say? <u>I just got home and realized this milk is sour.</u>

   What would you like to see happen? <u>I would like a new carton of milk.</u>

2. You took a suit to the dry cleaners and it came back with a stain on it. Who would you talk to?

   _____

   What would you say?

   _____

   What would you like to see happen?

   _____

3. You paid cash for your meal in a restaurant, but the server did not bring back your change. Who would you talk to?

   _____

   What would you say?

   _____

   What would you like to see happen? _____

4. There is a charge on your credit card bill for something that you didn't buy. Who would you talk to?

   _____

   What would you say?

   _____

   What would you like to see happen?

   _____

C With a partner, choose one of the situations in Exercise B and write a conversation between the customer and the representative of the business. Practice your conversation and present it to the class.

D One of the most effective ways to complain about a product or service is to write a business letter. Read the letter below.

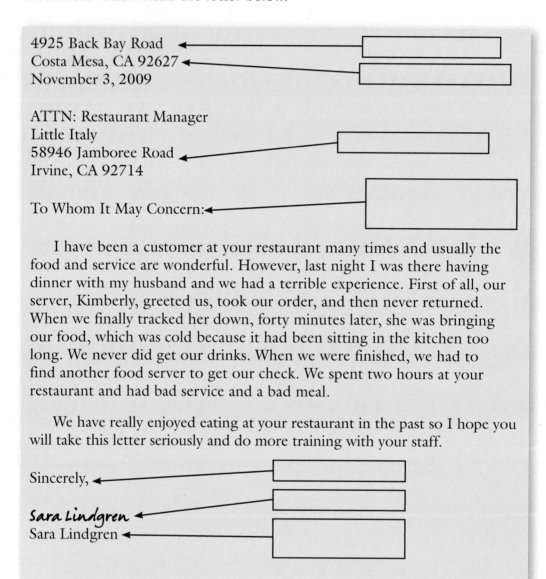

4925 Back Bay Road
Costa Mesa, CA 92627
November 3, 2009

ATTN: Restaurant Manager
Little Italy
58946 Jamboree Road
Irvine, CA 92714

To Whom It May Concern:

    I have been a customer at your restaurant many times and usually the food and service are wonderful. However, last night I was there having dinner with my husband and we had a terrible experience. First of all, our server, Kimberly, greeted us, took our order, and then never returned. When we finally tracked her down, forty minutes later, she was bringing our food, which was cold because it had been sitting in the kitchen too long. We never did get our drinks. When we were finished, we had to find another food server to get our check. We spent two hours at your restaurant and had bad service and a bad meal.

    We have really enjoyed eating at your restaurant in the past so I hope you will take this letter seriously and do more training with your staff.

Sincerely,

Sara Lindgren
Sara Lindgren

E Answer the questions about the letter.

1. Who is Sara complaining to? _____

2. What is she complaining about? _____

3. What do you think will happen? _____

Vocabulary   Grammar
Life Skills
Academic   Pronunciation

 Use these words to label the parts of the business letter on page 34.

- return address
- date
- address
- greeting/salutation

- body
- closing
- typed/printed name
- signature

 A business letter should contain certain information. Look at Sara's letter again. Did she mention all of these pieces of information in her letter?

- who she is
- why she is writing
- an explanation of the problem or situation
- a satisfactory resolution

H Choose one of these situations and write a business letter to make a complaint. Don't forget to format the letter correctly and include all of the necessary information.

Company	Reason for Letter
1. Lane's Accessories 8695 Tiguk Ave. Sioux Falls, SD 57104	The purse you bought is falling apart after one month.
2. Media Vision 4679 Lolly Lane Long Beach, CA 90745	You were charged for two months of cable instead of one.
3. Riverview Bank 47986 Washington Ave. Grand Rapids, MI 49503	There is a charge on your credit card statement that doesn't belong to you.
4. Produce World 875 7th Ave. New York, NY 10011	You were treated poorly by an employee.
5. (your own idea)	(your own idea)

Review

A Imagine that your family of four has $3,000 to live on per month. Realistically, how would you budget your money? Fill in the chart. (Lesson 1)

Monthly Expense	Budgeted Amount
Rent / Mortgage Payment	
Utilities	
Auto: Car Payment /Gas/ Insurance	
Food	
Medical	
Clothing	
Entertainment	
TOTAL	$3,000

B Look at the budget below. Calculate the differences and totals. (Lesson 1)

Monthly Expense		Budgeted Amount	Actual Amount Spent	Difference
Auto	Car Payment	$404.00	$404.00	
	Insurance	$72.39	$72.39	
	Gas	$180.00	$179.90	
	Maintenance	$100.00	$29.99	
Housing	House Payment	$1,490.00	$1,490.00	
	Utilities	$122.00	$110.75	
	Phone (home, cell)	$150.00	$230.00	
Food	Groceries	$350.00	$345.00	
	Eating Out	$200.00	$215.00	
Other	Clothing	$350.00	$224.59	
	Entertainment	$300.00	$315.03	
	Medical	$100.00	$40.00	
	TOTAL			

C What are three things you can do to be a smart consumer? (Lesson 2)

1. _____

2. _____

3. _____

D Imagine that you have just inherited $100,000 from a relative. What would you do with it? Write three conditional statements about the possibilities. Then, share your answers with the class. (Lesson 2)

1. If I inherited $100,000, I would _____

   _____

2. _____

   _____

3. _____

   _____

E Write *credit card*, *loan*, or *both* for each statement. (Lesson 3)

1. You need to apply for this.   _____

2. This can be used to buy an expensive item.   _____

3. You need collateral for this.   _____

4. This often has an annual fee.   _____

5. Sometimes this has an introductory offer.   _____

6. You will pay a penalty if your payment is late.   _____

7. This has an interest rate that
   affects your payments.   _____

8. You can get this from the bank.   _____

F List three advertising techniques that are used to get you to buy a product. (Lesson 4)

1. _____

2. _____

3. _____

G Imagine that you are writing an advertisement for a product. What information should be included in your ad? Make a list and share it with the class. (Lesson 4)

Review

H Complete each sentence with the passive form of the verb in parentheses. (Lesson 4)

1. Camcorders _____ (sell) at electronics stores.

2. Advertisements _____ (create) to sell products.

3. Advertisers _____ (pay) to convince you to buy certain products.

4. Sometimes an ad _____ (write) to confuse you.

I What four things should be included in a business letter that expresses a complaint? (Lesson 5)

1. _____

2. _____

3. _____

4. _____

J Decide if each statement is true or false, based on what you learned in this unit. If the statement is false, rewrite it to make it true. (Lessons 1-5)

____ 1. A smart consumer asks a lot of questions about a product before buying it.

_____

____ 2. Advertisements always tell you everything about the product.

_____

____ 3. Budgets are only for people with a lot of money.

_____

____ 4. It is better to pay cash for something if you can.

_____

____ 5. Sometimes credit cards carry high interest rates.

_____

____ 6. Writing a business letter is a good way to express a complaint.

_____

____ 7. You must have a credit card to buy an expensive item.

_____

My Dictionary

Make your own dictionary of the new words that you are learning in this class.

1. Buy a ruled notebook.
2. Divide the notebook into 26 sections—one for each letter of the alphabet.
3. As you learn new words, write them in your dictionary in the correct section.
4. After each word, write the page number where the word appears in your book, the definition, and an example sentence.

Go through Pre-Unit, Unit 1, and Unit 2. Make a list of twelve words that were new to you. Put them in alphabetical order below.

1. _____   5. _____   9. _____

2. _____   6. _____   10. _____

3. _____   7. _____   11. _____

4. _____   8. _____   12. _____

Now add these words to your dictionary.

Learner Log

In this unit, you learned many things about personal finance. How comfortable do you feel doing each of the skills listed below? Rate your comfort level on a scale of 1 to 4.

1 = Need more practice   **2** = OK   **3** = Good   **4** = Great!

Life Skill	Comfort Level				Page
I can calculate monthly expenses.	1	2	3	4	_____
I can plan a monthly budget.	1	2	3	4	_____
I know how to be a smart consumer.	1	2	3	4	_____
I can discuss purchasing options.	1	2	3	4	_____
I can interpret credit card and loan information.	1	2	3	4	_____
I can analyze advertising techniques.	1	2	3	4	_____
I can express consumer complaints.	1	2	3	4	_____
I can write a business letter.	1	2	3	4	_____

If you circled 1 or 2, write down the page number where you can review this skill.

Reflection

1. I learned _____.

2. I would like to find out more about _____.

Team Project

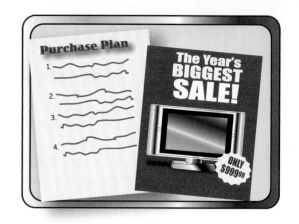

Create a purchase plan.

With a team, you will create a purchase plan for a large item.

1. Form a team with four or five students. Choose positions for each member of your team.

POSITION	JOB DESCRIPTION	STUDENT NAME
Student 1: **Team Leader**	See that everyone speaks English and participates.	
Student 2: **Secretary**	Take notes. Write down purchase plan.	
Student 3: **Designer**	Design ad for product and purchase plan layout.	
Student 4: **Spokesperson**	Report information to the class. Prepare team for the presentation.	
Student 5: **Assistant**	Help the secretary and designer with their work.	

2. Decide on a large item that your team would like to purchase.

3. Create an advertisement for this product.

4. Write down all the steps you will need to take to purchase this item. (*Hint:* think about a budget, comparison shopping, ads, loan information)

5. Write a brief description of how you will complete each step.

6. Design a purchase plan poster that has a space for the ad, each step in your purchase plan, and artwork.

7. Present your purchase plan to the class.

Buying a Home

GOALS

- ➤ **Interpret housing advertisements**
- ➤ **Compare types of housing**
- ➤ **Identify housing preferences**
- ➤ **Identify the steps to buying a home**
- ➤ **Interpret mortgage information**

LESSON 1

The American dream

GOAL ➤ Interpret housing advertisements

A Read the advertisements of homes for sale. Which name goes with which description? Write the names from the box above the correct description.

> Suburban Dream   Country Cottage   Downtown Condominium

HOMES FOR SALE

Cozy two-bedroom, two-bath, single-family home. Located in a secluded neighborhood, far from city life.

You won't believe this price for a house in this area.
Working fireplace.
Big yard.
Excellent seasonal views.
Must sell. Come see and make an offer now!
$240,000

★★★★★★★★★

Single-family, 4-bedroom, 3-bath, 2500 sq. ft. home with an added family room. Needs some loving care.
Location is great!
Near jobs, bus, and schools. You must see this home and area.

Amenities: pool, fireplace, central a/c, built-in master suite and big yard!

Let's negotiate!
Asking price
$325,000

RENTAL SALES

This 1000-square-foot condo is owned by the original owner and you'd think it was brand-new! Located in the heart of Los Angeles near all the nightlife you could imagine. Seller just added new carpet, new paint, new faucets and sinks, and beautiful ceramic tile flooring. Two master suites, indoor laundry room, detached two-car garage and large patio area. This condo will not last long on the market, so hurry!
$300,000

B Real estate agents write advertisements to get you excited about a property. What do you think the following phrases from the ads could mean? Write your own definitions.

asking price _____

brand-new _____

cozy _____

master suite _____

near nightlife _____

needs loving care _____

seasonal views _____

secluded _____

C The words in the box below describe the process of buying a home. Find each word in the ads on page 41 and try to work out the meaning by using the context. Then, discuss the meanings with a partner.

> offer   market   negotiate   amenities

D Look back at the ads on page 41 and complete the chart.

	Type of Property	Size	Asking Price	Number of Bedrooms	Number of Bathrooms	Location	Amenities
Country Cottage							big yard, fireplace, view
Suburban Dream	single-family home						
Downtown Condominium		1,000 sq. ft.					

E Listen to the advertisements of homes for sale and fill in the information you hear.

CD 1
TR 9

<u>Prince's Palace</u>

Price: _____

Size: _____

Neighborhood:

_____

Amenities: _____

_____

<u>Fixer-Upper</u>

Price: _____

Size: _____

Neighborhood:

_____

Amenities: _____

_____

<u>City High-Rise</u>

Price: _____

Size: _____

Neighborhood:

_____

Amenities: _____

_____

<u>Rural Residence</u>

Price: _____

Size: _____

Neighborhood:

_____

Amenities: _____

_____

 F Using the vocabulary you have learned in this lesson, write an advertisement for the place where you live now. Draw or paste in a picture.

Bigger? Better?

GOAL ➤ **Compare types of housing**

CD 1
TR 10

A Listen to Joey and Courtney discuss two properties that Courtney looked at. As you listen, take notes about the advantages and disadvantages of each place.

House	Advantages	Disadvantages
	closer to job	
Condominium		

B With a partner, compare the house and the condominium.

EXAMPLE: *Student A:* What's an advantage of living in the house?
　　　　　　Student B: The house is larger than the condo.

C Which one would you rather live in? Why? Explain your reasons to a partner.

D Complete the chart with a partner.

Adjective	Comparative	Superlative
beautiful	more beautiful	the most beautiful
noisy	noisier	the noisiest
safe		
comfortable		
far		
friendly		
cheap		
big		

* Note: Some two-syllable adjectives have two forms; for example, *quieter* or *more quiet*.

E Write the adjective(s) from Exercise D that corresponds to each rule.

1. Add -*er* or -*est* to one-syllable adjectives. _____cheap_____

2. Use *more* or *the most* before two-syllable adjectives. _____

3. Add -*r* or -*st* to one-syllable adjectives that end in *e*. _____

4. Change *y* to *i* and add -*er* or -*est*. _____

5. Some adjectives have irregular forms. _____

6. Double the final consonant of adjectives ending in the pattern

of consonant-vowel-consonant and add -*er* or -*est*. _____

F Describe the place you live in now and compare it to a place that you used to live in. Use the adjectives from Exercise D.

EXAMPLE: I used to live in a small, one-bedroom apartment with uncomfortable furniture. Now I live in a bigger apartment with the most comfortable couch in the world!

G Listen to Sara and Courtney talk about homes that Sara has looked at recently.

CD 1
TR 11

Courtney: Have you looked at any new houses this week?
Sara: Yes, I looked at three places the other day. Look at this brochure!
Courtney: The *Country Cottage*, the *Suburban Dream*, and the *Downtown Condominium*. I like the sound of the *Country Cottage* best. It sounds more comfortable than the others.
Sara: Yeah, and it's the closest to where we live now.
Courtney: Oh really? Which place is the safest?
Sara: Actually, I think the *Suburban Dream* is the safest.
Courtney: Which one has the biggest floor plan?
Sara: The *Suburban Dream*. It would be ideal for our family.
Courtney: Is it the most expensive?
Sara: Why, of course! I have expensive taste.

H What questions does Courtney ask? How does Sara answer her? Practice the conversation with a partner.

GOAL ➤ **Compare types of housing**

I Study the charts with your teacher.

Questions Using Comparative and Superlative Adjectives				
Question word	**Subject**	**Verb**	**Adjective or Noun**	**Rule**
Which	one place house	is	bigger? closer to work? the safest?	Use *be* when following the verb with an adjective.
		has	more rooms? the biggest floor plan?	Use *have* before a noun.

Long and Short Answers			
Question	**Short answer**	**Long answer**	**Rules**
Which one is bigger, the condominium or the house?	The condominium.	The condominium is bigger. The condominium is bigger than the house.	• When talking about two things and mentioning both of them, use *than*.
Which place has more rooms?	The house.	The house has more rooms. The house has more rooms than the condominium.	• When talking about two things, but only mentioning one of them, do not use *than*.

J Write four comparative questions about the homes Joey and Courtney talked about in Exercise A.

EXAMPLE: _Which place is closer to Courtney's job?_

1. _____

2. _____

3. _____

4. _____

K With a partner, practice asking and answering the questions you wrote in Exercise J.

L Write sentences on a piece of paper comparing a place you used to live in to the place you live in now.

EXAMPLE: My old house had more bedrooms than the house I live in now.

LESSON 3

Housing preferences

GOAL ➤ Identify housing preferences

CD 1
TR 12

A **Think about these questions as you listen to the story about the Bwarie family.**

1. Why is the Bwarie family looking for a new home?

2. What are they looking for in a new home?

The Bwarie family has outgrown their apartment. They have three children and a baby on the way, and they are now renting a two-bedroom house. They've been putting away money every month from their paychecks, and they finally have enough money for a down payment on a house. Every Sunday, the whole family piles into the car and goes to look at properties for sale. So far, they have been doing this on their own, but now it's time to find a realtor.

However, before they meet with a realtor, they need to decide exactly what they want. Courtney and Joey Bwarie have thought long and hard about what they want to purchase. First of all, they want a house in a safe neighborhood that is within walking distance to the school that their children attend. Second of all, they want four bedrooms, one for Courtney and Joey, one for the two boys, and another for their daughter and the baby girl who will be born next month. The fourth room will be used as an office for Courtney, who works out of the home. As far as bathrooms, four would be ideal, but they could survive with three if they had to. Some other things they would like are a big backyard for the children to play in and an attached two-car garage. Other amenities, such as air-conditioning or a pool, are not important to them.

Now they know what they are looking for in a new home. That was the easy part. Finding the home . . . that's a different story!

B **Read the story again. Try to work out the meanings of these words and expressions by using the context.**

down payment	on the way	outgrown
pile into	putting away	realtor
within walking distance	works out of the home	ideal
survive	thought long and hard	

C **Go over the meanings of the words and expressions with your teacher. Then, choose three of the words or expressions and use them in sentences.**

D What are the Bwaries looking for in a home? Complete the checklist with as much information as you can based on the story in Exercise A.

Housing Preferences Checklist				
Features	**Yes**	**No**	**Features**	**Preference**
air-conditioning	❏	❏	type of property	
backyard	❏	❏	number of bathrooms	
balcony	❏	❏	number of bedrooms	
garage	❏	❏	location	
heating	❏	❏	price range	
pool	❏	❏	down payment (percentage)	

E What information on the checklist did the Bwaries not talk about? What do you think their preferences might be regarding these items?

F When asking someone about their preferences, you can use *yes/no* questions. Study the chart below.

Yes/No Questions and Answers		
Do you want	air-conditioning?	Yes, I do.
	a backyard?	No, I don't.
Do they need	a balcony?	Yes, they do.
	a garage?	No, they don't.
Does the house have	heating?	Yes, it does.
	a pool?	No, it doesn't.

Pronunciation

Yes/No Questions:

Rising Intonation

➤ Do you want a yard?

➤ Do you want five bedrooms?

➤ Does the house have a pool?

➤ Does it have a balcony?

G Practice asking and answering *yes/no* questions with a partner. Use the information in Exercise D.

EXAMPLE: *Student A:* Do they want air-conditioning?
Student B: No, they don't.

H Information questions start with *who, what, where, when, why,* or *how*. Study the chart.

Information Questions			
Information	**Example questions**		
type of property	What type	of property	do you want? is it?
number of bathrooms number of bedrooms	How many	bedrooms bathrooms	do you want? does it have?
location	Where		is it?
price range	What		is your price range?
down payment (percentage)	How much		can you put down?

I Practice asking and answering information questions with a partner. Use the information from the chart in Exercise D.

EXAMPLE:
Student A: What type of property do they want?
Student B: They want a house.

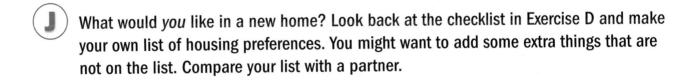

Pronunciation

Information Questions:
Rising and Falling Intonation

➤ What type of property do you want?

➤ How much can you put down?

➤ When will you be moving?

J What would *you* like in a new home? Look back at the checklist in Exercise D and make your own list of housing preferences. You might want to add some extra things that are not on the list. Compare your list with a partner.

LESSON **4**

Step-by-step

GOAL ➤ Identify the steps to buying a home

A What are some ways to find a house? With a group, list your ideas.

B Read the letter that Joey wrote to Paradise Realty.

15236 Dahlia Avenue
Costa Mesa, CA 92627
February 13, 2008

Paradise Realty
9875 Timber Lane
Costa Mesa, CA 92627

Dear Paradise Realty:

My family has decided to purchase a new home, and we would appreciate any information you can send us about homes for sale.

We are looking for a four-bedroom home. We would like to live in a safe neighborhood, close to our children's school. We would prefer a home with a big enclosed yard that our children can play in. We might want to build a pool in the future, but right now it is not a priority. Other amenities, such as air-conditioning, central heating, and closet space would be nice, but they are not essential.

Our price range is between $300,000 and $350,000, and we are prepared to put down 10%. Please contact me at the address above or you may call me or my wife, Courtney, at (949) 555-2408. Thank you for your time.

Sincerely,

Joseph Bwarie
Joseph Bwarie

 C Read the steps for buying a home and put them in the correct order. Write a number next to each sentence.

___ Apply for a loan.
___ Choose a home you'd like to buy.
___ Decide how much money you can spend.
___ Decide what you are looking for.
___ Have the home inspected.
___ Make an offer on the home.
___ Move in.
___ Negotiate until both parties come to an agreement.
___ Start looking for homes in a neighborhood you'd like to live in.

D Now read the article about home buying and check your answers.

BUYING A HOME

Home buyers can spend up to three months, and possibly more, looking for and purchasing a home. Their search begins by looking at housing ads, driving through neighborhoods they are interested in, and walking through open houses. Many first-time buyers will meet with a real estate agent to get help finding and buying a home.

Home buyers should know how much they can afford before they start looking for a home. It isn't worth your time to look for a new home if you can't really afford to buy one. So, it's a good idea to look at your financial situation first. You might be surprised how much money you can borrow, especially if the interest rates are good. Also, if you have some money for a down payment, your monthly payments may be lower than you think.

You should never make an offer on a home without looking at other houses in the same neighborhood. Just as you would comparison shop for a car or computer, you should do a cost comparison on different homes for sale. You can do this by asking about the recent sales of similar properties, which any real estate agent can tell you. Also, if you can find something out about the seller and his or her motivation for selling, it will put you in a better position to negotiate. For instance, maybe the seller needs to sell quickly and would accept a low offer.

Once you have found the property that you want and can afford, you are ready to make an offer. A low-ball offer is an offer that is much lower than the asking price. Unless the house is really overpriced or the seller needs to sell it quickly, he or she will probably not accept a low-ball offer. Once you make an offer that is reasonable to the seller, he or she will either accept it or make a counter offer. If he or she makes a counteroffer, the negotiating process has begun. You may have to go back three or four times before an agreement is reached.

Being a good negotiator can be tricky. Take your time when making your decision. This is a very important decision and you don't want to be rushed. Sometimes you can negotiate for repairs to be done to the home before you move in, or you can ask the seller to pay for some of your closing costs. As soon as a written offer is made and accepted by both parties, the document becomes a legally binding contract.

One of the first things you do after the contract is agreed upon is to get a home inspection. You need to hire a paid professional inspector to inspect the home, searching for defects or other problems. The inspector usually represents the buyer and is paid for by the buyer. The contract that you sign with the seller protects you as a buyer by allowing you to cancel closing on the deal if an inspector finds problems with the property that the seller is unwilling to have fixed or give the buyer credit for.

Once the contract has been signed, the lender (usually a bank) starts processing the loan. Once all the inspections are done and any repairs are completed, the final papers for the transfer of the title are prepared. Finally, the closing takes place on the date agreed upon in the offer. On that date, the title comes to you and you can begin enjoying your new home!

E Find these words in the article and match them with the correct meaning.

___ 1. afford

___ 2. contract

___ 3. cost comparison

___ 4. negotiate

___ 5. lender

___ 6. motivation

___ 7. offer

___ 8. closing

a. a legal document

b. amount of money that buyer is willing to pay for a house

c. looking at different prices of homes

d. person or company that loans money

e. the desire to do something

f. when all papers are signed and titles are transferred

g. to have enough money to purchase something

h. discuss until you reach an agreement

F What are the benefits of owning your own home? What are the drawbacks? Discuss them with a partner.

G Write a paragraph summarizing the process of buying a home.

Financial planning

GOAL ➤ Interpret mortgage information

A Todd and Sara Mason are thinking of buying a house. Todd is worried about money, so he made an appointment with a financial planner to talk about a mortgage. Discuss the questions below with a partner.

1. What is a financial planner?

2. What do you think the financial planner will tell Todd and Sara about getting a mortgage? Make a list with a partner.

1. _____

2. _____

3. _____

4. _____

5. _____

CD 1
TR 13

B Listen to Todd talk to the financial planner. What does the financial planner say? Is anything he says on the list you made?

C Do you know what these words and expressions mean? Discuss them with your classmates and teacher.

mortgage	financial commitment	afford
get approved for a loan	price range	credit check
down payment	deposit	purchase price

 D Listen to the first part of the conversation again. What are the three questions Todd must ask himself? Write them below.

CD 1
TR 14

1. _____

2. _____

3. _____

 E What are the next steps Todd must take? Listen to what the financial planner says and write the four steps below.

CD 1
TR 15

1. _____

2. _____

3. _____

4. _____

 F Todd will need to give the financial planner six things. Do you remember what they are? Write them below. If you can't remember, listen again.

CD 1
TR 16

1. _____

2. _____

3. _____

4. _____

5. _____

6. _____

 G Imagine that you are trying to get a mortgage and you have to gather all of the items listed in Exercise F. Put a check mark (✓) next to each one that you have at home right now.

H   Now that Todd knows how to get a mortgage, he needs to learn about the different types of mortgages. Read about each type below.

Fixed-Rate Mortgages

A fixed-rate mortgage has a fixed interest rate for the life of the loan, which could be 10, 20, or 30 years. You will make the same payment every month for the life of the loan and, at the end of the term, your loan will be paid off. The advantage of this type of loan is the interest rate never changes and the monthly payment is always the same.

Adjustable Rate Mortgages

An adjustable rate mortgage (ARM) begins like a fixed-rate mortgage with a fixed interest and a constant monthly payment, but this mortgage will adjust after a certain amount of time, anywhere from six months to five years. At this point, the interest rate and your monthly payment will change based on the market at the time. Furthermore, every month the rate and payment could change based on how the market changes.

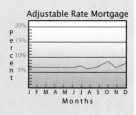

Balloon Mortgages

A balloon mortgage has a fixed interest rate and a fixed monthly payment, but after a certain amount of time, for example five years, the entire balance of the loan is due. This is a short-term loan, usually for people who can't qualify for a fixed-rate mortgage or an ARM.

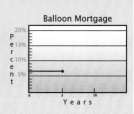

I   Using the information from Exercise H, put a check mark (✓) in the correct column(s).

	Fixed-Rate	ARM	Balloon
1. The monthly payment is always the same.			
2. The interest rate changes after a certain period of time.			
3. The interest rate is fixed.			
4. The monthly payment will change based on the market.			
5. This type of loan is short term.			

J   If you were going to buy a house, which type of loan would you get? Why?
Write a short paragraph about your preference.

A Read the housing advertisements and complete the chart below. (Lesson 1)

1. Always wanted to take a house and make it your own? Here's your chance! Settle into this 4-bedroom, 3.5 bath, 2,000-square-foot fixer-upper: $250,000. Located in a busy neighborhood with lots of other families, this place is perfect for a young family.

2. Move out of the slow life and into the fast lane! A beautifully spacious, 1,200-square-foot studio apartment at the top of one of the city's newest sky-rises is just what you're looking for. The building has 24-hour security. Utility room with washers and dryers is in the basement. The owner wants to lease it for $2,000 a month but will sell for $700,000. Hurry! This one will go fast!

3. You've finally decided it's time to move out of the city and into the country. Well, we've got just the place for you. This 3-bedroom, 3-bathroom rural residence is just what you need. It's a spacious, 5,000-square-foot, ranch-style home with a huge backyard and pool. It's located at the end of a cul-de-sac with only five other homes. It is now being offered at $600,000.

	Type of Property	Size	Asking Price	Number of Bedrooms	Number of Bathrooms	Location	Amenities
Home 1							
Home 2							
Home 3							

B Look at the housing ads on page 56. Complete the sentences by circling the correct verb and using the comparative or superlative form of the word in parentheses. (Lesson 2)

1. Home #3 (is /(has)) _____more space_____ than Home #2. (space)

2. Home #2 (is / has) _____. (expensive)

3. Home #2 (is / has) _____ than Home #1. (amenities)

4. Home #1 (is / has) _____ than Home #2. (big)

5. Home #3 (is / has) _____. (large)

6. Home #1 (is / has) _____ than Home #3. (bathrooms)

7. Home #2 (is / has) _____. (security)

8. Home #3 (is / has) _____ than Home #2. (spacious)

9. Home #2 (is / has) _____ than Home #1. (small)

10. Home #1 (is / has) _____ than Home #3. (bedrooms)

C Complete the housing preferences checklist based on what you would want in a home. (Lesson 3)

Housing Preferences Checklist				
Features	Yes	No	Features	Preference
air-conditioning	❏	❏	type of property	
backyard	❏	❏	number of bathrooms	
garage	❏	❏	number of bedrooms	
heating	❏	❏	location	
pool	❏	❏	price range	

D Write four *yes/no* questions you could ask someone about his or her housing preferences. (Lesson 3)

1. _____

2. _____

3. _____

4. _____

Review

E Write four information questions you could ask someone about his or her housing preferences. (Lesson 3)

1. _____

2. _____

3. _____

4. _____

F Now ask a partner the questions you wrote in Exercises D and E and complete the checklist below based on his or her answers. (Lesson 3)

Housing Preferences Checklist				
Features	**Yes**	**No**	**Features**	**Preference**
air-conditioning	❑	❑	type of property	
backyard	❑	❑	number of bathrooms	
garage	❑	❑	number of bedrooms	
heating	❑	❑	location	
pool	❑	❑	price range	

G Put the steps to buying a home in the correct order (1–10). (Lesson 4)

____ Start looking at ads in the newspaper and looking in neighborhoods you'd like to live in.

____ Negotiate with the seller until you come to an agreement.

____ Move in.

____ Make an offer on a home.

____ Get the title to the house transferred into your name.

____ Get a home inspection.

____ Find the home you want to buy.

____ Figure out how much money you can spend.

____ Decide on your housing preferences.

____ Apply for a loan.

H Take turns describing the process of getting a mortgage with a partner. Then, discuss the three different types of mortgages. (Lesson 5)

My Dictionary

Making lists of words that are related to each other can help you recall them when you need them. For example, in this unit you learned new words related to buying a home. Complete the lists below with related words from this unit.

Housing Ads	Buying a Home	Mortgages
cozy	home inspection	fixed-rate

Add these lists to the back of the dictionary that you started in Unit 2. (Save some pages in the back for more vocabulary lists.) Add the words that are new to you to your dictionary with definitions and examples.

Learner Log

In this unit, you learned many things about buying a home. How comfortable do you feel doing each of the skills listed below? Rate your comfort level on a scale of 1 to 4.

1 = Need more practice   **2** = OK   **3** = Good   **4** = Great!

Life Skill	Comfort Level	Page
I can interpret housing advertisements.	1 2 3 4	_____
I can use context clues to understand vocabulary.	1 2 3 4	_____
I can write an advertisement.	1 2 3 4	_____
I can compare properties.	1 2 3 4	_____
I can complete a housing preferences checklist.	1 2 3 4	_____
I can explain the steps to buying a home.	1 2 3 4	_____
I can interpret mortgage information.	1 2 3 4	_____

If you circled 1 or 2 of the skills, write down the page number where you can review these skills.

Reflection

1. I learned _____.

2. I would like to find out more about _____.

Team Project

Create a real estate brochure and decide on a property to buy.

Form a team with four or five students. Choose positions for each member of your team.

HOMES FOR SALE

Let's Negotiate!
Asking price just
$225,000
Single-family 4-bedroom, 3-bath, 1500 sq. ft., home with an added family room. Near jobs, bus, and schools. You must see this home and area. Amenities: pool, fireplace, central a/c, master suite and big yard!

Cozy, two-bedroom, two-bath, single-family home. Located in select neighborhood, far from city life.

You'd think this 1,000-square foot condo was brand new! Located in the heart of Los Angeles, near all the nightlife you can imagine. Seller just added new carpet, paint, new faucets and sinks, and beautiful ceramic tile flooring. Two master suites, laundry room, underground parking, balcony with spectacular views. This condo will not last long on the market, so hurry!

$200,000

You won't believe this price for a house in this area. Working fireplace, big yard, excellent seasonal views. Must sell. Come see and make an offer now!
$120,000

POSITION	JOB DESCRIPTION	STUDENT NAME
Student 1: **Team Leader**	See that everyone speaks English and partcipates.	
Student 2: **Writer**	Write advertisements. Write list of preferences and questions.	
Student 3: **Designer**	Design a brochure.	
Students 4/5: **Realtors**	Represent the real estate agency.	

Part 1: With an advertising team, you will create a real estate brochure.

1. Create an imaginary real estate agency. What is the name of your agency?
2. Come up with three houses that your agency is trying to sell. Make a brochure for these properties, including pictures and brief advertisements. Display your brochure in the classroom.

Part 2: As a family, you will choose which properties you are interested in, meet with a realtor and decide which property to purchase.

1. As a family, decide what your housing preferences are and make a list.
2. From the brochures posted around the room, choose two properties that you are interested in, each one from a different agency.
3. Prepare a list of questions that you'd like to ask about each property.
4. In teams of two or three, set up appointments with the realtor and meet with them about the properties you are interested in purchasing.
5. Report back to your group and make a decision about which property you'd like to make an offer on.
6. Make an offer on the property.

Community

GOALS

➤ Locate community resources
➤ Use the telephone
➤ Give suggestions

➤ Interpret a road map
➤ Identify ways to volunteer
in the community

LESSON 1

Your community

GOAL ➤ Locate community resources

Where is Consuela?
What information can she find here?

 A Consuela Sanchez is at the Loronado Welcome Center. She needs some help.
Read the conversation.

Consuela: Hi. We just moved to <u>Loronado</u> and I'm looking for a place
to <u>get a job</u>. Can you help me?
Receptionist: Of course. Why don't you try the <u>Employment Development Department</u>?
It's located on <u>Orange Avenue</u>.
Consuela: Great! Thanks.

 B With a partner, practice the conversation in Exercise A, but change the <u>underlined</u>
information. Use the expressions below and information you know about your community.

1. take some English classes
2. get a bus schedule
3. use a computer
4. volunteer
5. check out some books

6. get medical help
7. register my little boy for school
8. go swimming
9. look at some art
10. sign up for baseball

Do you know if there is a library near here?
Can you show me where Orange Avenue is?
Can you tell me when the post office opens?

C In each question in the box above, there are actually two questions. Can you find them? Write them below.

EXAMPLE: Do you know if there is a library near here?

1st question: **Do you know?**

2nd question: **Is there a library near here?**

1. Can you show me where Orange Avenue is?

1st question: _____

2nd question: _____

2. Can you tell me when the post office opens?

1st question: _____

2nd question: _____

D When two questions are combined into one, it is called an *embedded question*. One question is embedded in the other. Study the chart.

Embedded Questions		
Introductory question	**Embedded question**	**Rules**
Can you show me	where *Orange Avenue is?*	In an embedded information question, the subject comes before the verb.
Do you know	if there is a library near here?	For *yes/no* questions, use *if* before the embedded question.
Can you tell me	when the library opens?	For questions with *do* or *does*, take out *do/does* and use the base form of the verb.
Why do we use embedded questions? They sound more polite than direct questions.		

GOAL ➤ **Locate community resources**

Common Expressions Used to Introduce Embedded Questions	
Would you tell me . . . ?	Will you show me . . . ?
Can you explain . . . ?	Do you know . . . ?

E Change these questions to embedded questions using the expressions from the box.

EXAMPLE: What is the name of the local adult school?

Do you know what the name of the local adult school is?

1. What is the address of the public pool?

_____

2. Where is Loronado?

_____

3. Do you sell running shoes?

_____

4. What time does the library close?

_____

5. Is Orange Adult School on this street?

_____

6. When do classes begin?

_____

7. Where do you take your cans and papers for recycling?

_____

8. Is your restaurant open on Sunday evenings?

_____

F On a piece of paper, write five embedded questions that you could ask a school counselor.

EXAMPLE: Can you explain how to get a high school diploma?

Can you tell me . . . ?

GOAL ➤ Use the telephone

A What phone number would you call if you wanted information about the following items? Look at the directory below and write the correct number on the line.

1. getting a driver's license   555-0013

2. a bus schedule

3. a place to borrow books

4. medical help

5. school registration for your teenage son

6. swim lessons

7. looking at some art

8. a place for your daughter to skate after school

9. contesting your parking ticket

10. activities for your grandparents

Community Resources

Balboa Park Museum
555-2939   71852 Orange Ave

Bus Transit
555-2678   35984 First Street

Chamber of Commerce
555-4671   72064 Orange Ave

City Clerk
555-8403   63246 Fifth Street #1

Department of Motor Vehicles
555-0013   54679 Fourth Street

Employment Development Department
555-5334   94678 Orange Avenue

Health Clinic
555-8473   26489 First Street

High School
555-1238   34658 Loro Road

Hospital
555-7623   79346 Orange Ave

Little League Baseball
555-7300   66554 Third Street

Orange Adult School
555-9134   46589 Fourth Street

Public Library
555-0507   34661 Loro Road

Public Pool
555-4499   56321 Third Street

Senior Center
555-7342   97685 Sixth Street

Skate Park
555-6482   35211 Fourth Street

Superior Court
555-1796   96345 Orange Avenue

Village Elementary School
555-8462   34660 Loro Road

CD 1
TR 17

B Listen to the phone conversations. Who did each person call? What information did he or she want?

1. Place: Bay Books

Information: store hours

2. Place: _____

Information: _____

3. Place: _____

Information: _____

4. Place: _____

Information: _____

5. Place: _____

Information: _____

C Sometimes it is helpful to write down what you want to say before you make a phone call. For each of the examples above, write what you might say when the person answers the phone.

1. Hi. Could you please tell me your store hours? _____

2. _____

3. _____

4. _____

5. _____

D Using the questions you wrote above, practice short conversations with a partner. Change the underlined information for each item you wrote in Exercise C. Take turns being the clerk who answers the phone.

EXAMPLE: *Clerk:* Thank you for calling *Bay Books.* How can I help you?

You: *Hi. Could you please tell me your store hours?*

  (**E**) **Read and listen to the conversation.**

CD 1
TR 18

Host: Thank you for calling Scott's Steakhouse. How can I help you?
Caller: Yes, I was wondering if you are open for lunch.
Host: Yes, we are open for lunch from 11 A.M. to 3 P.M.,
Monday through Friday.
Caller: Do I need reservations?
Host: Reservations are not necessary, but we recommend them
during the busy lunch hours.
Caller: Great. Thanks for your help!
Host: You're welcome. Goodbye.
Caller: Bye.

 (**F**) **Practice the conversation in Exercise E with a partner.**

Pronunciation

Annunciation and Intonation

➤ When you are talking on the telephone, it is important that you
pronounce every word very clearly (annunciate) and speak with rising
and falling intonation. This is important because the person on the
other end of the line can't see your mouth or your facial expressions.
Try to remember this tip as you do the exercises below.

 (**G**) **Walk around the classroom and talk to four different classmates. Using the information
below, have conversations like the one in Exercise E.**

Calling	Information Needed	Response
Paris French Bistro	if reservations are needed and if there is a dress code	yes yes—coat and tie for men; no jeans for women
Loronado High School	location of the school's talent show	Coast Community Church at 11341 Fifth Street
Community Center	days and times of concerts in the park	every Sunday from 1–4 P.M.
Loronado Public Library	age required to get a library card	age five with parent's signature

Why don't we . . . ?

GOAL ➤ **Give suggestions**

Where are Consuela and her husband?
Who are they talking to?

 A **Consuela and her husband, Ricardo, are talking to their next-door neighbors. Read their conversation.**

Ricardo: Let's find a good Italian restaurant. Can you think of where we could go?

Jim: Why don't we try this great little place called Island Pasta? It's a local hangout and I've heard the food is great!

Marie: I think they're closed tonight. How about going to Laredo's for a Mexican meal instead?

Consuela: Great idea!

Making Suggestions	Responding to Suggestions
Why don't we . . . ? We could . . . How about . . . ? Do you want to . . . ? Let's . . .	Great idea! Yes, let's do that! Sure! How about . . . instead.

 B **With a partner, make new conversations. Use the topics below and suggestions from the chart. Talk about places in your community.**

1. a good shoe store
2. a good movie for kids
3. a nice restaurant for your best friend's birthday dinner
4. a bookstore with a large selection of books
5. a good place to find really fresh fruit and vegetables
6. a place to eat Mexican food
7. a place to listen to good music
8. a bookstore to buy the required book for class

GOAL ➤ **Give suggestions**

C Read the notices on the community bulletin board. Which notice is the most interesting to you? Why?

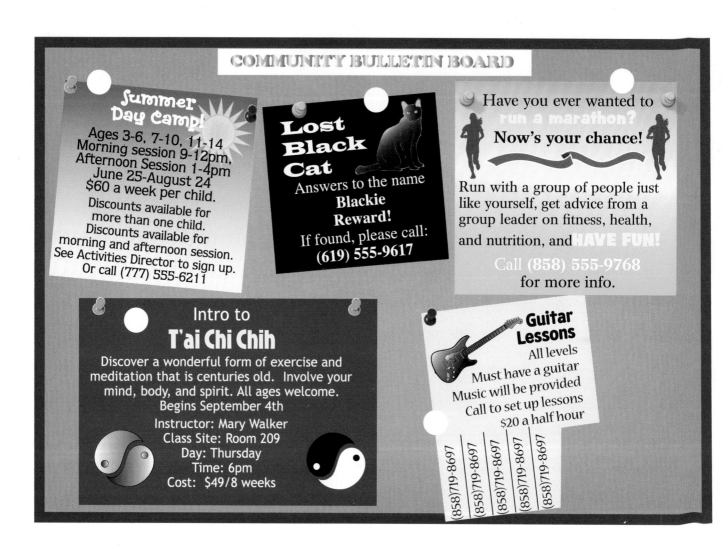

COMMUNITY BULLETIN BOARD

Summer Day Camp!
Ages 3-6, 7-10, 11-14
Morning session 9-12pm,
Afternoon Session 1-4pm
June 25-August 24
$60 a week per child.
Discounts available for more than one child.
Discounts available for morning and afternoon session.
See Activities Director to sign up.
Or call (777) 555-6211

Lost Black Cat
Answers to the name
Blackie
Reward!
If found, please call:
(619) 555-9617

Have you ever wanted to **run a marathon? Now's your chance!**
Run with a group of people just like yourself, get advice from a group leader on fitness, health, and nutrition, and **HAVE FUN!**
Call **(858) 555-9768** for more info.

Intro to
T'ai Chi Chih
Discover a wonderful form of exercise and meditation that is centuries old. Involve your mind, body, and spirit. All ages welcome.
Begins September 4th
Instructor: Mary Walker
Class Site: Room 209
Day: Thursday
Time: 6pm
Cost: $49/8 weeks

Guitar Lessons
All levels
Must have a guitar
Music will be provided
Call to set up lessons
$20 a half hour
(858) 719-8697
(858) 719-8697
(858) 719-8697
(858) 719-8697
(858) 719-8697

CD 1
TR 19

D Listen to the community members. Where can they find the information they need? Write the correct number next to each notice.

COMMUNITY BULLETIN BOARD

Arts and Crafts

Ever wanted to
learn how to knit?
Do needlepoint?
Make gifts for friends?
Help your children with art projects?
Come join our craft group on Saturday
mornings. There is a $5 material fee each day
you attend.

Come this Saturday!

For more information, call Rick (858) 555-8693

Summer Volleyball League

Got a group of people who
want to play volleyball?
Want to join a team that
needs another player?
Sign up for our summer
volleyball league!
All league games are on
Tuesday nights.
For more information,
call (777)555-7809

B22

Did you hear your number?

Bingo Sunday nights
starting 4pm.
Call Charlene
for more info
(619) 438-9728

Basketball-Open Gym

The new downtown
Recreation Center
is where the action is!
Come on down Mondays and
Wednesdays afternoon from 5-7pm
and join a game.
Recreation Center
4350 Third Street, (777)555-6211

Roommate wanted
Female, non-smoker
1 bed, 1 bath, kitchen, garage
$400 + sec. deposit.
Call Laura (619) 555-9475.

(619) 555-9475
(619) 555-9475
(619) 555-9475
(619) 555-9475
(619) 555-9475

BOOK CLUB

Do you like
mysteries? Fiction?
Romance?
Non-fiction?
Suspense?
Come down to
the Book Barn
and join one of
our book clubs! Read
a book every month
and meet with others
who share your
passion to discuss it!
Book Barn,
4212 Loro Road,
Tel. (777) 555-5630

E Work in pairs. Student A: Make a statement about one of the notices
on the community bulletin board. Student B: Respond with a suggestion.

EXAMPLE: *Student A:* I need a place to send my kids for the summer while I'm at work.
Student B: Why don't you phone the Summer Day Camp?
Student A: That's a good idea.

F Make a community bulletin board in your classroom. Think of things you could offer
and make flyers.

How far is it?

GOAL ➤ **Interpret a road map**

A A legend helps you read the symbols on a road map. Write the correct words from the box next to the symbols.

✈ _____   ③ _____

Ⓗ _____   ⑤ _____

Ⓐ _____   ⑧ _____

⦙ _____   🛏 _____

⑤ _____   Ⓡ _____

> airport
> hospital
> campground
> exit
> freeway
> interstate
> state highway
> state scenic highway
> hotel/motel
> rest area

B Look at the map on page 71 and answer these questions with a partner.

1. Is there a hospital in Rose?
2. What interstate has rest areas?
3. Where is the nearest campground to Grandville?
4. Which highways are scenic?
5. Is there an airport near Lake Ellie?

C Look at the highway map scale and estimate the road distances on the map on page 71.

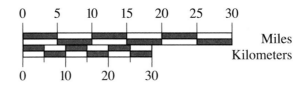

1. How far is it from Grandville to Rose?
2. How far is it from Poppington to Lake Ellie?
3. How far is it from Loronado to Poppington?
4. How far is it from Lake Ellie to Rose?
5. How far is it from Grandville to Poppington?
6. How far is it from Rose to Loronado?

GOAL ➤ Interpret a road map

CD 1
TR 20

D Listen to the people giving directions. Where will the driver end up? Fill in the circle next to the correct answer.

1. ○ Grandville   ○ Rose   ○ Lake Ellie   ○ Loronado   ○ Poppington

2. ○ Grandville   ○ Rose   ○ Lake Ellie   ○ Loronado   ○ Poppington

3. ○ Grandville   ○ Rose   ○ Lake Ellie   ○ Loronado   ○ Poppington

4. ○ Grandville   ○ Rose   ○ Lake Ellie   ○ Loronado   ○ Poppington

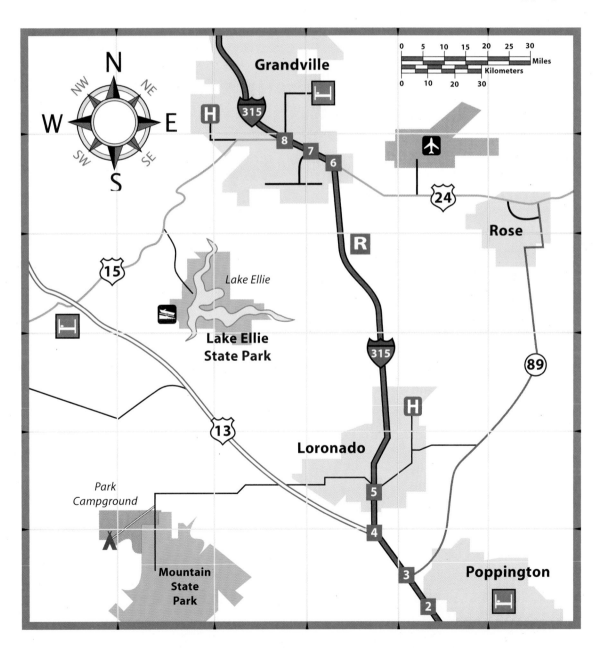

Conversation Strategy: Repeat for Clarification

When you are getting important information from someone, such as directions, it is always a good idea to ask for clarification. Asking for clarification means repeating back what was said or asking the other person to repeat it so you can double-check what you wrote down. One way to do this is to repeat just the part of the sentence that you are unsure of.

EXAMPLES: *A:* Take the freeway exit and veer left.
  B: Veer left?
  A: Yes.

  A: Take 605 to 405 to 22.
  B: Did you say 605 to 405 to 22?
  A: Yes.

 Now practice giving and receiving directions with a partner. Student A: Look at the map on page 71 to give directions. Student B: Write down what your partner says. If you get confused, ask your partner to slow down or repeat for clarification. Then, change roles.

EXAMPLE: From Rose to Grandville
  Student A: I live in Rose and I need to get to Grandville. What's the best way to get there?
  Student B: Take 24 East to 315 North. Follow 315 North to the third exit.
  Student A: About how far is it?
  Student B: Sixty miles.
  Student A: Thank you so much.

1. Poppington to Lake Ellie
2. Loronado to Poppington
3. Lake Ellie to Rose
4. Rose to Loronado
5. Grandville to Poppington

 Now look at the directions you wrote down when you were Student B. Compare them to the map. Are they correct?

Volunteering

GOAL ➤ **Identify ways to volunteer in the community**

 Have you ever offered to help a friend or family member do something? Have you ever done something for your neighbor? Do you belong to any local community organizations where you help out in some way? If you answered *yes* to any of these questions, you are a volunteer!

 Look at the pictures. Where do you think these people are volunteering? Write your ideas on the line beneath each picture.

1. _____

2. _____

3. _____

4. _____

5. _____

6. _____

7. _____

8. _____

9. _____

C Before you volunteer, you need to think about what you would like to do or what you are good at. Look at the list below and check (✓) the things that you like to do and are good at. Add your own ideas to the bottom of the list.

Skills	I can . . .	I like to . . .	My partner can . . .	My partner likes to . . .
ask for money				
build structures				
clean				
cook				
give a speech				
keep track of money				
make decorations				
make phone calls				
organize				
plan a meeting				
plan a party				
put books in alphabetical order				
spend time with children				
talk to people				
teach someone English				
teach someone to read				
teach someone math				
use the computer				

D Now interview a partner. Ask him or her what he or she likes to do and put check marks (✓) in the appropriate columns. Use these question beginnings: *Can you . . . ? Do you like to . . . ?*

LESSON 5

GOAL ➤ Identify ways to volunteer in the community

E What are some places in your community you might be able to volunteer? With a group, make a list. Share your list with the class.

Places to Volunteer

F Now look back at the checklist on page 74. Come up with two places where you and your partner might like to volunteer based on your skills and preferences.

Places Where I Can Volunteer	Places Where My Partner Can Volunteer
1.	1.
2.	2.

G Now that you have two places where you can volunteer, what's the next step? With your partner, come up with four questions you might ask when you visit or call the location.

1. Can I speak to the person in charge of volunteering?

2. _____

3. _____

4. _____

H Now practice asking your questions to a partner. Imagine that your partner works at the place where you want to volunteer. Your partner will have to be creative and come up with answers to your questions.

A In your community, where would you go to do the following things? Write one idea on each line. (Lessons 1–2)

1. get a bus schedule _____

2. borrow books _____

3. get a flu vaccine _____

4. take an art class _____

5. use a computer for free _____

B Change the questions below to embedded questions. (Lesson 1)

1. What is the address of the library?

_____

2. Do you sell vitamins?

_____

3. What time does the museum close?

_____

4. Is the Adult School on this street?

_____

5. When do classes begin?

_____

C Imagine you are calling the places that you wrote down in Exercise A. With a partner, practice having telephone conversations about each of the topics listed. (Lesson 2)

EXAMPLE: get a bus schedule

Receptionist: Transit Authority, can I help you?
Caller: Yes, I was wondering how I can get a bus schedule.
Receptionist: Well, you can come down to our office and pick one up or you can go online and print out a schedule of any route you want.
Caller: Really? Oh, that's a great idea. I'll use my computer to print out a schedule. Thanks!
Receptionist: You're welcome.

D Imagine that you just moved into your neighborhood. Write four questions you might ask your new neighbors about different places to go. Then, practice asking and answering the questions with a partner. Write the suggestions that your partner gives you in the chart below. (Lessons 1–3)

Questions	Suggestions
1. Do you know of a good coffee shop?	1. Why don't you try the Happy Kettle on 4th street?
2.	2.
3.	3.
4.	4.
5.	5.

E Now ask your partner to give you directions from the school to the four places he or she suggested. Write down the directions. Ask for clarification to double check them with your partner. (Lesson 4)

1.

2.

3.

4.

Review

F Read the map and answer the questions. (Lesson 4)

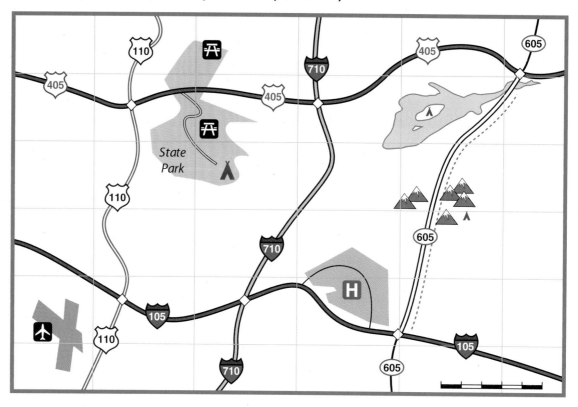

1. What highway would you take to get to the hospital? _____

2. What highway would you take to get to the state park? _____

3. Which highways run north-south? _____

4. How would you get from the lake to the hospital? _____

_____

G List three things you like to do. For each thing you like to do, write two places where you could volunteer. (Lesson 5)

Things That I Like To Do	Places Where I Could Volunteer
1.	1. 2.
2.	1. 2.
3.	1. 2.

My Dictionary

Brainstorm a list of new words that you learned in this unit.

_____   _____

_____   _____

_____   _____

_____   _____

Sometimes one of the easiest ways for you to learn a new word is to write down the translation from your native language. For each word you wrote above, write its translation.

Now look back through the dictionary that you started in Unit 2. Write translations for all the words and expressions that are in there.

Learner Log

In this unit, you learned many things about community. How comfortable do you feel doing each of the skills listed below? Rate your comfort level on a scale of 1 to 4.

1 = Need more practice   **2** = OK   **3** = Good   **4** = Great!

Life Skill	Comfort Level				Page
I can identify resources in a community.	1	2	3	4	_____
I can ask about resources in a community.	1	2	3	4	_____
I can use the telephone.	1	2	3	4	_____
I can use embedded questions to ask for information.	1	2	3	4	_____
I can read a community bulletin board.	1	2	3	4	_____
I can make suggestions.	1	2	3	4	_____
I can interpret a road map.	1	2	3	4	_____
I can give and understand driving directions.	1	2	3	4	_____
I can volunteer in my community.	1	2	3	4	_____

If you circled 1 or 2, write down the page number where you can review this skill.

Reflection

1. I learned _____.

2. I would like to find out more about _____.

Create a community resource guide.

With a team, you will create a community resource guide. This project can be done in two ways:

1. Each team creates its own guide.
2. Each team creates a portion of a guide and all parts are combined at the end to make a class guide.

1. Form a team with four or five students. Choose positions for each member of your team.

POSITION	JOB DESCRIPTION	STUDENT NAME
Student 1: **Team Leader**	See that everyone speaks English and participates.	
Student 2: **Writer**	Take notes and write information for guide	
Student 3: **Designer**	Design and add art to guide.	
Students 4/5: **Spokespeople**	Report information to the class. Prepare team for the presentation	

2. As a class, decide what information should go in your guide(s), such as the names of local services, medical facilities, restaurants, events, and places to volunteer. Make a list on the board.

3. Decide if each team will create its own guide or if each team will work on a portion of a class guide. (If the second option is chosen, decide what section each team will work on.)

4. Create your guide or portion of the class guide. Each portion should include addresses, phone numbers, basic information, and a map. (Use the phone book or the Internet if you need to.)

5. Put your guide together.

6. Present your guide or portion of your guide to the class.

Health

GOALS

➤ Identify health habits
➤ Describe symptoms of illnesses
➤ Interpret doctor's instructions

➤ Interpret nutrition information
➤ Complete a health insurance form

LESSON **1**

Health habits

GOAL ➤ Identify health habits

A What are these people doing? Which activities are healthy? Which activities are unhealthy? Make two lists below.

Healthy Habits	Unhealthy Habits

B Can you think of other healthy and unhealthy habits? Add them to your lists.

C   Look at each health habit in the chart below and decide if it is healthy or unhealthy. Put a check mark (✓) in the correct column.

Health Habit	Healthy	Unhealthy
watching a lot of TV		
doing puzzles		
drinking too much alcohol		
drinking water		
eating fruits and vegetables		
eating junk food		
lifting weights		
meditating		
playing sports		
reading		
sleeping		
smoking		
spending time with friends and family		
taking illegal drugs		
walking		

D   There are two different types of health—mental health and physical health. Mental health is anything related to your mind and psychological well-being. Physical health is anything related to your body, both from a fitness and nutritional standpoint.

Look at the health habits you checked as healthy in the chart above. Decide which type of health each one benefits and write it in the correct column in the chart below.

Mental Health	Physical Health
doing puzzles	

 E Ms. Tracy's students took a poll in their class to find out what bad health habits they have. They presented their results in a bar graph. Read the bar graph and answer the questions.

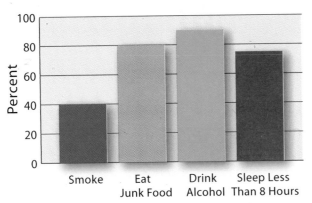

The Bad Health Habits of Ms. Tracy's Class

How to Calculate Percentage
1. First, find out the total number of students in your class.
2. Then divide the total number of students into the number of students who answered the question yes.
EXAMPLE: In a class of 25 students, 15 students exercise.

$$\begin{array}{r} .60 \\ 25\overline{)15.00} \\ \underline{15.00} \\ 0 \end{array}$$

3. Move the decimal over two places to the right to get the percentage.

.60 = 60%

1. What percentage of students eats junk food? ____

2. What percentage of students sleeps less than eight hours? ____

3. What percentage of students *doesn't* smoke? ____

4. What percentage of students *doesn't* drink alcohol? ____

5. What is the worst health habit Ms. Tracy's class has? ____

F With a group of students, list four good health habits. Take a poll in your class to see who practices these health habits. Make sure you ask everyone. Make a bar graph of your findings.

EXAMPLE: health habits—exercise poll
question: Do you exercise?

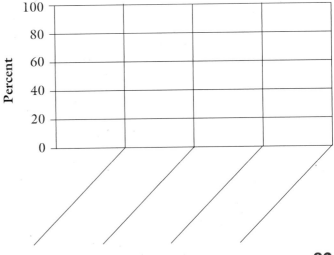

The Good Health Habits of My Class

What's the problem?

GOAL > Describe symptoms of illnesses

Who are the people in the picture?
What are they saying?

 Read the conversation between the doctor and the patient.

Doctor: Hello, John. What seems to be the problem?
John: <u>I've been coughing a lot</u>.
Doctor: Anything else?
John: Yes, <u>my chest has been hurting</u>, too.
Doctor: It sounds like you might have <u>bronchitis</u>. I'd like to do some tests
to be sure, and then I'll give you a prescription to relieve your symptoms.
John: Thanks, Doc.

 Practice the conversation with a partner. Then, practice the conversation several more times, replacing the underlined parts with the information below.

Symptom 1	Symptom 2	Diagnosis
1. I've been blowing my nose a lot.	My body has been aching.	common cold
2. My leg's been hurting.	I haven't been walking properly.	muscle spasm
3. I've been throwing up.	I've been feeling faint and dizzy.	flu

C Study the chart with your teacher.

Present Perfect Continuous	
Example	**Form**
I *have been resting* for three hours.	*Affirmative sentence*: *has/have* + *been* + present participle
He *hasn't been sleeping* well recently.	*Negative sentence*: *has/have* + *not* + *been* + present participle
How *long have they lived/have they been living* here?	*Question*: *has/have* + subject + *been* + present participle

- To emphasize the duration of an activity or state that started in the past and continues in the present. Example: The president *has been sleeping* since 9 A.M.
- To show that an activity has been in progress recently. Example: You've *been going* to the doctor a lot lately.
- With some verbs (*work, live, teach*), there is no difference in meaning between the present perfect simple and the present perfect continuous. Example: They *have lived/have been living* here since 2000.

Note: Some verbs are not usually used in the continuous form. These include *be, believe, hate, have, know, like,* and *want*.

D Complete the sentences using the present perfect continuous form of the verbs in parentheses and suitable time expressions.

for + period of time	*since* + point in time
two weeks	Tuesday
five days	5:30 P.M.
a month	1964
a long time	last night
a while	I was a child

1. We _____have been going_____ (go) to our family doctor for ____a long time____.

2. The kids _____ (sleep) since _____.

3. The couple _____ (practice) medicine in Mexico for _____.

4. I _____ (work) at the same job for _____.

5. How long _____ (you, study) to be an optometrist?

6. Satomi _____ (feel well / not) since _____.

7. The boy _____ (cough) since _____.

8. Enrico _____ (take) his medicine for _____.

9. Minh _____ (think) about changing jobs for _____.

10. They _____ (go) to the gym together for _____.

E Now review the present perfect simple with your teacher.

Present Perfect Simple	
Example	**Form**
He *has seen* the doctor. I *have moved* four times in my life.	<u>Affirmative sentence</u>: *has/have* + past participle
They *haven't been* to the hospital to see her.	<u>Negative sentence</u>: *has/have* + *not* + past participle OR *has/have* + *never* + past participle
Have you *written* to your mother?	<u>Question</u>: *has/have* + subject + past participle

- When something happened (or didn't happen) at an unspecified time in the past.
  Example: She *has* never *broken* her arm.
- When something happened more than once in the past (and could possibly happen again in the future). Example: I *have moved* four times in my life.
- When something started at a specific time in the past and continues in the present.
  Example: They *have lived* here for ten years.

F Choose the present perfect simple or the present perfect continuous form of the verbs in parentheses. In some sentences, you will also need to decide if *for* or *since* should be used.

1. They _____ (be) to their new doctor several times.

2. Marco _____ (have) asthma _____ 1995.

3. She _____ (give) me a lot of help _____ I moved here.

4. I _____ (see / not) the dentist _____ a year.

5. _____ (you / see) the new hospital downtown?

6. _____ (you / wait) _____ a long time?

7. Santiago _____ (miss) two appointments this week.

8. We _____ (cook) _____ three hours.

9. He _____ (examine / not) her _____ she was a child.

10. How long _____ (you / know) Maria?

G Work in groups of three or four. Ask and answer questions beginning with *How long*. Use the present perfect simple or present perfect continuous.

EXAMPLES: How long have you been going to the same doctor?
How long have you had a headache?

What did she say?

GOAL ➤ Interpret doctor's instructions

What are these people talking about?
What do you think they are saying?

CD 1
TR 21

A The doctor tells Rosa several important things about her health at her checkup. Listen and number the sentences in the correct order (1–5).

____ "I can give you some more tests."

____ "The most important thing is to stay active."

____ "You'll have to come back in two weeks."

____ "If you start exercising more, your cholesterol should go down."

____ "If you don't stop eating junk food, you will have serious health problems."

CD 1
TR 22

B Now listen to Rosa reporting her conversation to her friend. Fill in the missing words.

1. She said she __would__ give ___me___ some more tests.

2. The doctor told me the most important thing _____ to stay active.

3. She told me if _____ _____ exercising more, _____ cholesterol should go down.

4. She said if _____ _____ stop eating junk food, _____ _____ have serious health problems.

5. She said _____ _____ to come back in two weeks.

C What differences do you notice between the sentences in Exercise A and Exercise B? Study the chart with your teacher.

Direct Speech	Indirect Speech	Rule
"You have to exercise more."	The doctor *explained* (that) I had to exercise more.	• Change pronoun. • Change present tense to past tense.
"The most important thing is your health."	The doctor *said* (that) the most important thing was my health.	

GOAL ➤ Interpret doctor's instructions

Vocabulary | Grammar
Life Skills
Academic | Pronunciation

D Match the kinds of doctors with the type of treatment they provide.

obstetrician   podiatrist   chiropractor   dentist   pediatrician

  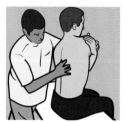  

E Read the statements and decide what kind of doctor said each one. Use indirect speech to tell your partner what each person said.

EXAMPLE: "Your child is in perfect health!"
The pediatrician said my child was in perfect health.

Indirect Speech Verbs	
announced	stated
answered	said
complained	explained
replied	agreed

1. "You need to brush your gums and floss your teeth every day."

2. "Your children are eating too many sweets and sugary foods. They need to eat more fruits and vegetables."

3. "It is a good idea to go to prenatal classes for at least three weeks."

4. "The shoes you are wearing aren't good for your feet."

5. "You'll hurt your back if you don't bend your knees to lift heavy objects."

6. "You need to make an appointment to have those cavities filled."

7. "You need to make sure you take your vitamins every day."

LESSON 3 **GOAL** ➤ **Interpret doctor's instructions**

F Study the chart.

Direct Speech	Indirect Speech
I want to lose weight.	I told *you* (that) I wanted to lose weight.
My test results are negative.	He notified *me* (that) my test results were negative.
It is important to check your heart rate.	My personal trainer said (that) it was important to check my heart rate.
I feel sick.	She complained (that) she felt sick.

- Some verbs are usually followed by an indirect object or pronoun. (*tell, assure, advise, convince, notify, promise, remind, teach, warn*)

- Some verbs are NOT followed by an indirect object or pronoun. (*say, agree, announce, answer, complain, explain, reply, state*)

 G Rewrite each quote using indirect speech with the subject and verb in parentheses.

EXAMPLE: "You need to walk for 30 minutes every day." (the doctor, remind)

<u>The doctor reminded me that I needed to walk for 30 minutes every day.</u>

1. "He needs to stop smoking." (the cardiologist, warn)

_____

2. "You have a very balanced diet." (the nutritionist, assure)

_____

3. "She is very healthy." (the pediatrician, agree)

_____

4. "You eat too much junk food." (the doctor, convince)

_____

5. "I read nutrition labels for every food I eat." (I, tell, the doctor)

_____

6. "We want to start exercising together." (our parents, announce)

_____

 H Think of a conversation you had with a doctor or health care professional. Tell your partner what the person said to you.

Nutrition labels

GOAL ➤ Interpret nutrition information

A Do you read the nutrition labels on the food that you buy? What do you look for? Why?

B Scan the nutrition label and answer the questions.

Nutrition Facts		
Serving Size 2 oz. (56gm)		
Servings Per Container 8		

Amount Per Serving

Calories 200		Calories from Fat 10

% Daily Value*

Total Fat 1g	2%
Saturated Fat 0g	
Cholesterol 0mg	
Sodium 0mg	
Total Carbohydrate 42g	14%
Dietary Fiber 2g	8%
Sugars 1g	
Protein 7g	

Vitamin A	0%
Calcium	0%
Thiamin	35%
Niacin	15%
Vitamin C	0%
Iron	10%
Riboflavin	15%
Folate	30%

*Percent Davily Values are based on a 2,000-calorie diet. Your daily values may be higher or lower depending on your caloric needs:

Calories		2,000	2,500
Total Fat	Less than	65g	80g
Sat Fat	Less than	20g	25g
Cholesterol	Less than	300mg	300mg
Sodium	Less than	2,400mg	2,400mg
Total Carbohydrate		300g	375g
Dietary Fiber		25g	30g

Calories per gram:
Fat 9   Carbohydrate 4   Protein   4

Ingredients: Semolina, Niacin, Iron, Thiamin Mononitrate, Riboflavin, Folic Acid

1. How much protein is in one serving of this product? _____

2. How many calories are in one serving of this product? _____ How many of those calories are from fat? _____

3. What vitamins and/or minerals does this product contain per serving?

   _____   _____

   _____   _____

   _____   _____

   _____   _____

4. How many carbohydrates are in one serving of this product? _____

5. How much fat is in one serving of this product? _____ How much of the fat is saturated? _____

6. How much of this product is one serving? _____

7. How many servings are in the box? _____

GOAL ➤ **Interpret nutrition information**

 C These words can be found on a nutrition label. (See the highlighted words on the nutrition label on page 90.) Write the correct letter next to each definition. Use each letter only once.

a. saturated fat   e. serving size   h. cholesterol
b. sodium   f. protein   i. vitamins
c. calories   g. ingredients   j. fiber
d. carbohydrates

_____ 1. This is the amount of food that a person actually eats at one time.

_____ 2. This is the amount of energy supplied by a kind of food.

_____ 3. This is a type of fat. It can contribute to heart disease.

_____ 4. This ingredient of food is not digested but it aids digestion.

_____ 5. This type of nutrient indicates the salt content of food.

_____ 6. This helps to build and repair muscles. It is found mainly in meat, fish, eggs, beans, and cheese.

_____ 7. These are whatever is contained in a type of food. On a nutrition label, they are presented in order of weight from most to least.

_____ 8. These are the best source of energy and can be found in breads, grains, fruits, and vegetables.

_____ 9. Eating too much of this can cause you to have heart disease and to be overweight.

_____ 10. These nutrients are found in food and help to keep your body healthy.

D How much do you know about the nutrients on food labels? Discuss the questions below with a small group.

1. Why is it good to read nutrition labels?

2. What do complex carbohydrates do for your body?

3. What does saturated fat do to your body?

4. What type of person should watch his or her sodium intake?

5. How much protein should you eat per day?

6. Why are simple carbohydrates good?

7. Why is it good to eat fiber?

GOAL ➤ Interpret nutrition information

Vocabulary
Grammar
Life Skills
Academic
Pronunciation

E Read the information about food labels.

Reading Nutritional Information on Food Labels

Knowing how to read the food label on packaged foods can help you build better eating habits. Here's a rundown of the basics you'll find on a food label and how you can use the information to improve your daily diet:

1. Serving Size The serving size on the label is supposed to be close to a "real-life" serving size—no more listing a teaspoon of salad dressing when most of us use a tablespoon. The information on the rest of the label is based on data for one serving. Remember, a package may contain more than one serving.

2. Calories The number of calories tells you how many calories are in one serving. The number of calories from fat tells you how many of those calories come from fat. Try to find foods with low amounts of calories from fat.

3. Fat This is where you look if you are trying to count fat grams. Total fat is important to watch, but saturated fat is particularly bad for you. Saturated fat raises your blood cholesterol level, which could lead to heart trouble.

4. Cholesterol Along with the saturated-fat information above, cholesterol amounts are important for anyone concerned about heart disease. High levels of cholesterol can lead to serious heart problems later in life.

5. Sodium Sodium (or salt) levels are important to monitor if you have high blood pressure.

6. Carbohydrates These fit into two categories—complex carbohydrates (dietary fiber) and simple carbohydrates (sugars). You want to eat more complex carbohydrates and fewer simple carbohydrates. Diets high in complex carbohydrates have been shown to fight cancer and heart disease. Simple carbohydrates are good for energy, but if you eat too many of them, you can expect your waistline to grow.

7. Fiber Fiber consists of complex carbohydrates that cannot be absorbed by the body. It aids digestion and can help lower blood cholesterol. High fiber foods include fruits, vegetables, brown rice, and whole-grain products.

8. Protein The food label doesn't specify a daily percentage or guideline for protein consumption because so much depends on individual needs. An athlete needs more than an office worker, but in a typical 2,000-calorie diet, most people need no more than 50 grams of protein per day.

9. Vitamins and Minerals The FDA requires only Vitamin A, Vitamin C, iron, and calcium amounts to be on food labels although food companies can voluntarily list others. Try and get 100 % of each of these essential vitamins and minerals every day.

10. Ingredients Ingredients are listed on food labels by weight from the most to the least. This section can alert you to any ingredients you may want to avoid because of food allergies.

F How much do you know about nutrition now? Decide if each statement is true or false. Fill in the correct circle.

	True	False
1. Reading food labels can improve your eating habits.	○	○
2. Diets high in complex carbohydrates can help fight cancer and heart disease.	○	○
3. Saturated fat lowers your blood cholesterol level.	○	○
4. You should watch your sodium intake if you have high blood pressure.	○	○
5. Most people need at least 100 grams of protein per day.	○	○
6. Simple carbohydrates are good for energy.	○	○
7. Foods with fiber can help lower cholesterol.	○	○

Do you want dental coverage?

GOAL ➤ **Complete a health insurance form**

A If you were looking for a good health insurance company, what things would you look for? Check (✓) the items below that would be most important for you. Share your answers with the class.

- ❑ dental coverage
- ❑ prescription plan
- ❑ vision plan
- ❑ low premium

- ❑ low deductible
- ❑ low co-pay
- ❑ good choice of providers
- ❑ good reputation

B Most insurance companies offer two types of coverage—HMO and PPO. What do these two terms stand for?

HMO: _____ _____ _____

PPO: _____ _____ _____

C What are the differences between an *HMO* and *PPO*? Work with a small group and write *HMO* or *PPO* on the line before each statement.

1. _____ higher out-of-pocket expenses

2. _____ low or sometimes free co-pay

3. _____ you can see any doctor you want to at any time

4. _____ you must choose one primary-care physician

5. _____ higher monthly premium

6. _____ lower monthly premium

7. _____ you must get a referral from your primary-care physician to see another doctor

8. _____ low or sometimes no out-of-pocket expenses

D Skim the health insurance application on this page and the next page. Put a check (✓) next to every part you can answer. Underline the parts you are not sure about.

Employee Applicant Information

First Name: _____ Middle Name: _____ Last Name: _____

Home Address:

Street: _____ City: _____ State: _____ Zip Code: _____

Sex: Male Female

Social Security Number: _____-_____-_____

Date of Birth: (mm / dd / yyyy) _____ / _____ / _____

Marital Status: ____ Married ____ Single

Work Phone: (_____) _____-_____ Home Phone: (_____) _____-_____

Job Title: _____

Hours Worked Per Week: _____

Annual Salary: _____

Tobacco: Have you or your spouse used any tobacco products in the past 12 months?

       Employee: ____Yes ____No   Spouse: ____Yes ____No

Dental: Do you want dental coverage? ____Yes ____No

Prescription Card: Do you want a prescription card? ____Yes ____No

Dependants: Dependants you want covered on this policy.

Spouse: _____

Date of Birth: (mm / dd / yyyy) _____ / _____ / _____ Sex: ____Male ____Female

Child #1 : _____

Date of Birth: (mm / dd / yyyy) _____ / _____ / _____ Sex: ____Male ____Female

Child #2: _____

Date of Birth: (mm / dd / yyyy) _____ / _____ / _____ Sex: ____Male ____Female

A-1: Within the last four (4) years, have you or any dependant received or been recommended to have treatment for any disorders or conditions of the following? Please check all that apply.

❑ Back   ❑ Stroke   ❑ Intestinal   ❑ Colon   ❑ Kidney   ❑ Muscular   ❑ Heart or Circulatory

❑ Cancer   ❑ Diabetes   ❑ Respiratory   ❑ Mental or Emotional   ❑ Liver

A-2: Within the last four (4) years, have you or any dependant used drugs not prescribed by a physician, been advised to have treatment or been treated for drug abuse, alcoholism or been a member of Alcoholics Anonymous?   Yes   No

A-3: Have you or any dependant ever had a positive blood test indicating HIV antibodies or been treated and/or advised by a medical practitioner as having Acquired Immune Deficiency Syndrome (AIDS), AIDS Related Complex (ARC), or any other immune system deficiency?   Yes   No

A-4: Have you or any dependant been hospitalized, had surgery, or had more than $5,000 in medical expenses in the last twelve (12) months? _____Yes _____No

A-5: Are you or any dependant pregnant? _____Yes _____No

If "Yes," what is your estimated due date? _____

A-6: Within the last four (4) years, have you or any dependant received or been recommended to have treatment for any disorders or conditions of the following? Please check all that apply.

❑ Ear   ❑ Hernia   ❑ Thyroid   ❑ Breast

❑ Eye   ❑ Allergy   ❑ Digestive System

❑ Joint   ❑ Asthma   ❑ Reproductive Organs

❑ Ulcer   ❑ Arthritis   ❑ High Blood Pressure

A-7: Within the last four (4) years, have you or any dependant received treatment or been advised to seek treatment for any reason not already mentioned? _____Yes _____No

Employee Name: _____

Date: (mm/dd/yyyy)_____ /____ /_____

E Work in pairs. Use a dictionary to help you understand the parts of the form that you underlined.

F Work with a small group to answer the following questions.

1. Why do you think health insurance companies need all of this information?
2. Why is it important to have health insurance?

G Now that you understand all the parts of the application, fill it out.
Note: If any information is too personal, just think about the answer and don't write it in your book.

Review

A In your opinion, what are the three most important good health habits to have? (Lesson 1)

1. _____

2. _____

3. _____

B In your opinion, what are the three worst health habits to have? (Lesson 1)

1. _____

2. _____

3. _____

C Complete the sentences using the present perfect simple or present perfect continuous form of the verb in parentheses. (Lesson 2)

1. I (not/eat) _____ meat for three years.

2. Sara (go) _____ to yoga classes since September.

3. Andres (drink) _____ two liters of water today.

4. I (not / sleep) _____ well recently.

5. I (never / smoke) _____ a cigarette.

6. Why (you / choose) _____ such a stressful job?

7. Marna (wheeze) _____ since last night.

8. We (see) _____ the same doctor for over ten years.

9. My father (have) _____ diabetes since he was a child.

10. The children (not / brush) _____ their teeth very well.

D Write the type of doctor you would see if you were having problems with the following. (Lesson 3)

1. feet   _____

2. back   _____

3. pregnancy   _____

4. baby's ears   _____

5. teeth   _____

E Change the sentences from direct speech to indirect speech. (Lesson 3)

1. "My daughter is sick."

   Maria said that _____.

2. "We won't be able to come to the meeting."

   Luis and Ricardo told me _____.

3. "They don't have time to go out."

   Hanif said _____.

4. "You need to take the medicine on an empty stomach."

   The doctor explained that _____.

5. "Your son is eating too much sugar."

   The pediatrician said _____.

6. "My back has been hurting for two months."

   I told the chiropractor _____.

7. "You need to take your prenatal vitamins every day."

   The obstetrician told me _____.

8. "Your husband needs to stay off his feet for a few hours a day."

   The podiatrist warned me _____.

Review

F Match the descriptions to the nutrition items. (Lesson 4)

1. ___ calories
2. ___ carbohydrates
3. ___ cholesterol
4. ___ saturated fat
5. ___ fiber
6. ___ ingredients
7. ___ protein
8. ___ serving size
9. ___ sodium
10. ___ vitamins

a. listed on a food label by weight
b. complex carbohydrates that cannot be absorbed by the body
c. salt
d. dietary fiber and sugar
e. try to get 100% of each every day
f. energy supplied by food
g. a type of fat that can contribute to heart disease
h. the amount of food a person eats at one time
i. helps build and repair muscles
j. too much of this could lead to heart disease

G What is important to you when looking for health insurance? Make a list. (Lesson 5)

_____

_____

_____

_____

_____

_____

_____

My Dictionary

Do you remember what you learned about word families in the Pre-Unit?
If not, look back at page P7 in Lesson 3 of the Pre-Unit.

Complete as much of the chart as you can with words from this unit. Then, complete the word families using your dictionary.

Noun	Verb	Adjective	Adverb
	advise		
insurance			XXXXX
	XXXXX	habitual	
medicine			

Look in your dictionary and see if any new words you have written down have other "family members." Add them to your dictionary.

Learner Log

In this unit, you learned many things about health. How comfortable do you feel doing each of the skills listed below? Rate your comfort level on a scale of 1 to 4.

1 = Need more practice   **2** = OK   **3** = Good   **4** = Great!

Life Skill	Comfort Level	Page
I can identify good and bad health habits.	1 2 3 4	_____
I can report illnesses and symptoms to a doctor.	1 2 3 4	_____
I can identify different types of doctors.	1 2 3 4	_____
I can tell someone what the doctor told me.	1 2 3 4	_____
I can identify vitamins and the nutritional content of foods.	1 2 3 4	_____
I can interpret and fill out health insurance forms.	1 2 3 4	_____

If you circled 1 or 2, write down the page number where you can review this skill.

Reflection

1. I learned _____.

2. I would like to find out more about _____.

Team Project

Create a community health pamphlet.

With a team, you will create a pamphlet to distribute to the community about good health practices.

1. Form a team with four or five students. Choose positions for each member of your team.

POSITION	JOB DESCRIPTION	STUDENT NAME
Student 1: **Team Leader**	See that everyone speaks English and participates.	
Student 2: **Writer**	Take notes and write information for pamphlet.	
Student 3: **Designer**	Design and add art to pamphlet.	
Students 4/5: **Spokespeople**	Prepare the team for presentation. Present pamphlet to the class.	

2. With your group, decide what information should go in your pamphlet, such as good health habits, types of doctors, nutrition, insurance information, etc.

3. Write the text and decide on the art to use in your pamphlet.

4. Put your pamphlet together.

5. Present your pamphlet to the class.

Getting Hired

GOALS

➤ Identify skills and characteristics
➤ Conduct a job search
➤ Write a resume
➤ Write a cover letter
➤ Prepare for a job interview

LESSON **1**

What skills do you have?

GOAL ➤ Identify skills and characteristics

Vocabulary · Grammar · Life Skills · Academic · Pronunciation

 A Look at the pictures. What jobs are these people doing? Discuss them with a partner.

 B A *skill* is something you can do, such as use a computer or write a report. What skills are required for each job above? Discuss your ideas with a small group.

GOAL ➤ **Identify skills and characteristics**

C Below is a list of job titles. Work in groups to write the job responsibilities that go with each job. Then, add two more job titles to the list.

Job Title	Job Responsibilities
accountant	
administrative assistant	
assembler	
business owner	
cashier	
computer technician	repairs computers
delivery person	
dental assistant	
electrician	
fire fighter	
garment worker	sews clothing
hairstylist	
homemaker	
landscape architect	
mail carrier	
receptionist	
reporter	
salesperson	
security guard	

D Practice the conversation below, using the information that you wrote in Exercise C.

Student A: What does a computer technician do?
Student B: A computer technician repairs computers.

E In groups, discuss the difference between skills and characteristics. A *skill* is something you can do, such as deliver mail or type a letter. A *characteristic* describes your personality and work habits, such as hardworking or well-organized. What are some other examples of characteristics?

GOAL ➤ **Identify skills and characteristics**

F Read some characteristics that employers look for in employees. Discuss the characteristics with your classmates and check (✓) the ones that describe you.

❑ a quick learner   ❑ creative   ❑ dependable
❑ detail-oriented   ❑ efficient   ❑ flexible
❑ good with numbers   ❑ great with people   ❑ hardworking
❑ well-organized   ❑ willing to accept responsibility   ❑ works well under pressure

G Read the descriptions and choose a characteristic to describe each person.

1. Suzanne works long hours and never takes any breaks. _____

2. You can always rely on Linh. _____

3. Li is always calm, even when it's very stressful. _____

4. You never have to explain anything to Vlasta twice. _____

CD 1
TR 23

H Listen to four people describe their skills, characteristics, and interests. Take notes in the first column. Then, suggest a job for each person in the second column.

Lam	Skills, characteristics, interests	Most suitable job
Lilia		
Morteza		
Hilda		

I Make a list of your skills and interests on a piece of paper. What are some jobs that you think you might enjoy and be good at? List at least three jobs. Then, list the characteristics you have that would make you good for each job.

Looking for a job

GOAL ➤ **Conduct a job search**

A What is the best way to look for a job? What are some different ways to look for a job? Make a list.

Ways to Look for a Job

B What are some things you need to think about before you begin your job search? Make a list.

1. hours available to work

2. _____

3. _____

4. _____

5. _____

6. _____

C When you find a job opportunity in a newspaper or on the Internet, what information is usually included? What information do you usually need to ask about? Look at the list below. Put each piece of information in the correct column.

benefits	job location	required skills
contact information	job title	salary/pay
how to apply	possibility of overtime	vacation
job hours	required qualifications	

Information Found in the Ad	Information I Need to Ask About
contact information	

GOAL ➤ **Conduct a job search**

D Think about the job you have now. (Some of you may be students or homemakers. If you are, these are your jobs. If you are retired, think about your last job.) Fill in the chart with information about your job.

	Information About Your Job
Job title	
Job location	
Job skills	
Qualifications	
Hours	
Salary	
Benefits	

E Interview your classmates about their jobs. Write questions for each piece of information, then ask your classmates the questions and complete the chart.

Interview Questions	**Classmate 1**	**Classmate 2**	**Classmate 3**
Title: What is your job title?			
Location:			
Skills:			
Qualifications:			
Hours:			
Benefits:			

F Imagine that you want to work for a company. It is important to find out some information about the company or business ahead of time. Fill in the chart.

What kind of information is useful to know?	Where can you find this information?
1. the number of employees who work for the company	1. in the company brochure on the company's website
2.	2.
3.	3.
4.	4.
5.	5.
6.	6.

G With a group of students, create your own company. Answer the questions below.

1. What does your company make or do?

2. Where is your company located?

3. How many people work for your company?

4. What are some of the job titles of people who work at your company?

5. What characteristics do you want your employees to have?

6. What do you pay your employees?

7. What hours do your employees work?

8. What benefits do you give your employees?

Resumes

GOAL ➤ Write a resume

 Read about Ranjit.

Ranjit Ghosh is from India. He moved to the United States seven years ago. In India, he attended the National Computer School and received a certificate in computer repair. His first job was troubleshooting computer repairs for a financial company. After he moved to the United States, he started assembling computers and was able to use the skills he had learned in his course in India. Although he loved his job, he needed another job to pay the bills. In addition to assembling computers, now he also repairs computers in the evenings for another company. Ranjit is busy, but he is doing what he loves.

 Answer the questions about Ranjit.

1. Ranjit has had three jobs. List them with the most recent first.

   a. _____

   b. _____

   c. _____

2. Where did he go to school and what did he receive? _____

   _____

3. Why does Ranjit have two jobs in the United States? _____

   _____

C **Think about your job history. List your jobs starting with the most recent first.**

1. _____   4. _____

2. _____   5. _____

3. _____   6. _____

GOAL ➤ **Write a resume**

D Read Ranjit's resume.

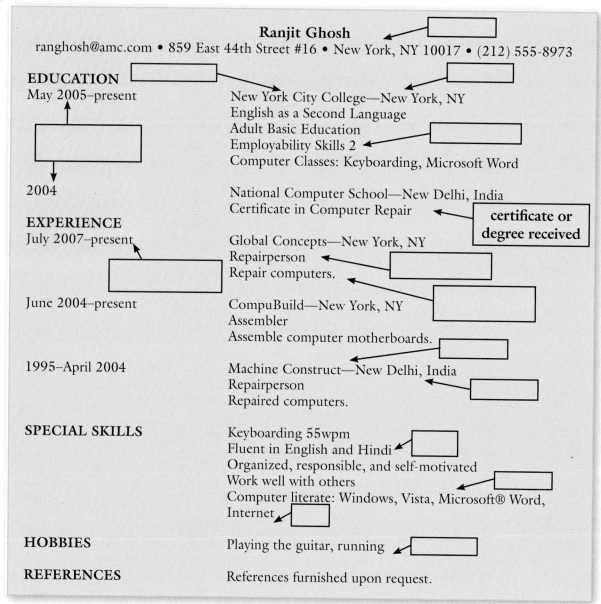

Ranjit Ghosh

ranghosh@amc.com • 859 East 44th Street #16 • New York, NY 10017 • (212) 555-8973

EDUCATION
May 2005–present

New York City College—New York, NY
English as a Second Language
Adult Basic Education
Employability Skills 2
Computer Classes: Keyboarding, Microsoft Word

2004

National Computer School—New Delhi, India
Certificate in Computer Repair

certificate or
degree received

EXPERIENCE
July 2007–present

Global Concepts—New York, NY
Repairperson
Repair computers.

June 2004–present

CompuBuild—New York, NY
Assembler
Assemble computer motherboards.

1995–April 2004

Machine Construct—New Delhi, India
Repairperson
Repaired computers.

SPECIAL SKILLS

Keyboarding 55wpm
Fluent in English and Hindi
Organized, responsible, and self-motivated
Work well with others
Computer literate: Windows, Vista, Microsoft® Word,
Internet

HOBBIES

Playing the guitar, running

REFERENCES

References furnished upon request.

E Can you identify the parts of a resume? Use the words below to label Ranjit's resume.

certificate or degree received	job title	name of company
computer skills	languages	name of school
dates of education	location of company	names of classes taken
dates of job	location of school	skills
job responsibilities	name and address	things you enjoy doing

F Look at the words in the box in Exercise E. Why is it important to put each of the pieces of information on your resume? Discuss the reasons with a group and make notes about each item.

G Think about your own resume. Fill in your information.

1. Schools you have attended: _____

_____

_____

2. Classes you have taken: _____

_____

_____

3. Certificates or degrees you have received: _____

_____

4. Awards you have received: _____

_____

5. Names and locations of companies you have worked for: _____

_____

_____

6. Job titles and responsibilities you have had: _____

_____

_____

7. Special characteristics you have: _____

_____

_____

8. Things you enjoy doing: _____

_____

_____

  H Using the information you wrote in Exercise G, write your resume on a piece of paper.

Cover letters

GOAL ➤ **Write a cover letter**

A What is the purpose of a cover letter? Read the cover letter that Ranjit sent in with his resume.

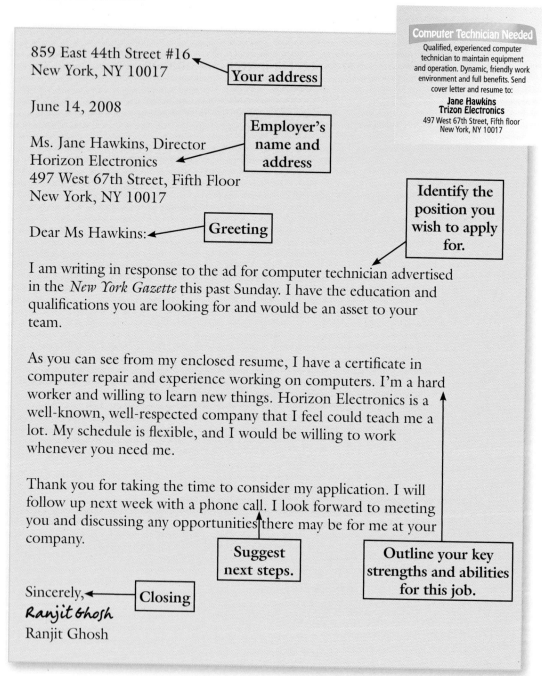

859 East 44th Street #16
New York, NY 10017 ◄— **Your address**

June 14, 2008

Ms. Jane Hawkins, Director
Horizon Electronics ◄— **Employer's name and address**
497 West 67th Street, Fifth Floor
New York, NY 10017

Dear Ms Hawkins: ◄— **Greeting**

I am writing in response to the ad for computer technician advertised in the *New York Gazette* this past Sunday. I have the education and qualifications you are looking for and would be an asset to your team. — **Identify the position you wish to apply for.**

As you can see from my enclosed resume, I have a certificate in computer repair and experience working on computers. I'm a hard worker and willing to learn new things. Horizon Electronics is a well-known, well-respected company that I feel could teach me a lot. My schedule is flexible, and I would be willing to work whenever you need me.

Thank you for taking the time to consider my application. I will follow up next week with a phone call. I look forward to meeting you and discussing any opportunities there may be for me at your company.

Suggest next steps.

Outline your key strengths and abilities for this job.

Sincerely, ◄— **Closing**
Ranjit Ghosh
Ranjit Ghosh

Computer Technician Needed
Qualified, experienced computer technician to maintain equipment and operation. Dynamic, friendly work environment and full benefits. Send cover letter and resume to:
Jane Hawkins
Trizon Electronics
497 West 67th Street, Fifth floor
New York, NY 10017

B Read the following job descriptions.

Company Name: Healthy Living (61835 Valley Road, Grand Rapids, MI 96837)
Company Description: A company that produces and sells vitamins.
Job Title: Warehouse Supervisor
Job Description: In charge of packaging orders in the warehouse. Must be able to supervise 20 employees. No experience with vitamins necessary, but warehouse experience would be helpful.

Company Name: Medical Valley Hospital (875 Washington Ave, Portland, OR 79468)
Job Title: Nurse's Aide
Job Description: Help the RNs take care of the patients. Fill out basic paperwork regarding patients, be able to take vital signs. No experience necessary—will train. Looking for someone who is friendly, patient, and doesn't mind working with sick people.

Company Name: Auto Land (75436 Harbor Blvd., Costa Mesa, CA 92627)
Company Description: Used car lot
Job Title: Salesperson
Job Description: Selling cars. Must be good with people and outgoing. No sales experience necessary.

Company Name: Choicemart (87645 Santa Maria, Houston, TX 77042)
Job Title: Customer Service
Job Description: Handling customer complaints, helping customer fill out proper paperwork to file complaint, entering the complaint information into the computer and setting up meetings to discuss the complaints with the proper department. Must have good oral and written communication skills. Must be good with people and have the ability to handle angry customers. Basic computer skills helpful.

Company Name: Villa Italia (756 Fifth Ave, New York, NY 06458)
Job Title: Food Server
Job Description: Serve food to customers. Must have restaurant experience, but serving experience not necessary. Will train.

C Choose one job that you would like to apply for from the descriptions in Exercise B. Tell your partner why you would be good for this job.

GOAL ➤ **Write a cover letter**

D Imagine that you are applying for the job that you chose in Exercise C. Write a cover letter to the company.

_____

_____

_____

_____

_____

_____

_____

_____,

_____

_____

_____

_____

_____

_____

_____

_____

 LESSON 5 **Interviewing**

GOAL ➤ Prepare for a job interview

A Now that you have written your resume and your cover letter, it's time to get ready for the interview! The best way to prepare for an interview is to practice.

Look at the sample interview questions below. How would you answer them? Discuss each question with a group, then write your answers on a piece of paper.

1. Tell me about yourself.

2. Why are you applying for this job?

3. Why do you think you would be good at this job?

4. What is your greatest strength?

5. What is your greatest weakness?

6. Do you prefer to work alone or with other people?

7. Why did you leave your last job?

8. What did you do at your last job?

9. What did you like most about your last job?

10. Describe a situation where you had a conflict with another employee. How did you solve it?

11. What special skills do you have that would benefit our company?

12. What characteristics do you have that would make you a good employee?

13. Do you have any questions?

 B With a partner, practice asking and answering the interview questions. Since you are just practicing, it is OK to look at the answers you wrote in Exercise A.

GOAL ➤ **Prepare for a job interview**

C In addition to your answers, job interviewers are also looking at other aspects of your interview. Read the list below. How would you rate yourself for each?

Handshake	○ Fair	○ Medium	○ Excellent
Appearance	○ Fair	○ Medium	○ Excellent
Eye contact with interviewer	○ Fair	○ Medium	○ Excellent
Voice level (volume)	○ Fair	○ Medium	○ Excellent
Facial expressions	○ Fair	○ Medium	○ Excellent
Posture / body position	○ Fair	○ Medium	○ Excellent
Self-confidence / comfort level	○ Fair	○ Medium	○ Excellent
Willingness to volunteer information	○ Fair	○ Medium	○ Excellent
Appropriateness of responses to questions	○ Fair	○ Medium	○ Excellent
Effectiveness in describing strengths, skills, and abilities	○ Fair	○ Medium	○ Excellent

D Looking at the list above, which two aspects are your strongest?

1. _____

2. _____

E Which two aspects do you need to work on the most?

1. _____

2. _____

F Now it's time to practice. You will be interviewing for the job that you wrote your cover letter for. Work with a partner. Take turns being the interviewer and the interviewee.

Student A: Interviewer
Ask your partner at least ten of the questions on page 113. When the interview is over, fill out the Mock Interview Evaluation Form on page 115 in you partner's book.

Student B: Interviewee
Do your best to answer the questions without looking at your notes and try to do well on each of the aspects listed in Exercise C.

LESSON 5

GOAL ➤ **Prepare for a job interview**

G Fill out the mock evaluation form about your partner.

MOCK INTERVIEW EVALUATION FORM

Name of applicant: _____

Name of interviewer: _____

Date of interview: _____

Job applied for: _____

Rate the applicant on each of the following questions by writing *excellent*, *good*, or *fair*.

What kind of impression did this person make? _____
Did the person give answers that would make an employer want to hire him or her?

_____

Did the person have a friendly, enthusiastic, and positive attitude?

_____

Rate the applicant on the criteria below on a scale of 1 to 5.
(1 = poor, 5 = excellent)

CRITERIA   **Rating**

What suggestions can you give this person for how to make a better impression?

CRITERIA	1	2	3	4	5
1. Handshake	___	___	___	___	___
2. Appearance	___	___	___	___	___
3. Eye contact with interviewer	___	___	___	___	___
4. Voice level (volume)	___	___	___	___	___
5. Facial expressions	___	___	___	___	___
6. Posture / body position	___	___	___	___	___
7. Self-confidence / comfort level	___	___	___	___	___
8. Willingness to volunteer information	___	___	___	___	___
9. Appropriateness of responses to questions	___	___	___	___	___
10. Effectiveness in describing strengths, skills, and abilities	___	___	___	___	___
11. Overall evaluation	___	___	___	___	___

Additional comments: _____

_____

_____

Review

A Write job responsibilities for the job titles. (Lesson 1)

Job Title	Job Responsibilities
administrative assistant	
cashier	
delivery person	
dental assistant	
electrician	
homemaker	
receptionist	
salesperson	

B List six characteristics you think an employer is looking for in an employee. (Lesson 1)

1. _____   4. _____

2. _____   5. _____

3. _____   6. _____

C Imagine you are looking for a job. Complete the table about your ideal job. (Lesson 2)

Information About Your Ideal Job	
Job title	
Job location	
Job skills	
Qualifications	
Hours	
Salary	
Benefits	

D List ten pieces of information that go on a resume. (Lesson 3)

1. _____

2. _____

3. _____

4. _____

5. _____

6. _____

7. _____

8. _____

9. _____

10. _____

E How would you answer these interview questions? Write your answers below. (Lesson 5)

1. What is your greatest strength? _____

_____

2. What is your greatest weakness? _____

_____

3. What special skills do you have that would benefit our company?

_____

_____

4. What characteristics do you have that would make you a good employee?

_____

_____

5. What did you like most about your last job?

_____

_____

Review

F If you want to get a job, what are all the things you need to do from beginning to end? List them below. (Lessons 2–5)

1. Write a resume. _____

2. _____

3. _____

4. _____

5. _____

6. _____

G In this unit, you learned many things about getting a job. With a group, discuss the following. Complete the sentences to explain why each one is important. Share your answers with the class. (Lessons 1–5)

1. Knowing what my skills are is important because _____

_____.

2. Finding information about the job I want is important because _____

_____.

3. Finding information about the company I am applying to is important because

_____

_____.

4. Writing a resume is important because _____

_____.

5. Writing a cover letter is important because _____

_____.

6. Practicing interviewing is important because _____

_____.

My Dictionary

Take out your dictionary and add a section about yourself.

Make two lists—one for your skills and one for your characteristics. Write down anything you can do and anything that describes you. If you need to add definitions for any of the words, put them in the same section.

Whenever you are applying for a job or applying for school, you can pull out these lists as a reference.

Learner Log

In this unit, you learned many things about getting hired. How comfortable do you feel doing each of the skills listed below? Rate your comfort level on a scale of 1 to 4.

1= Need more practice **2** = OK **3** = Good **4** = Great!

Life Skill	Comfort Level				Page
I can identify the characteristics of a good employee.	4	3	2	1	_____
I can identify job titles and skills.	4	3	2	1	_____
I can conduct a job search.	4	3	2	1	_____
I can write a resume.	4	3	2	1	_____
I can write a cover letter.	4	3	2	1	_____
I can prepare for a job interview.	4	3	2	1	_____
I can interview for a job.	4	3	2	1	_____

If you circled 1 or 2, write down the page number where you can review this skill.

Reflection

1. I learned _____.

2. I would like to find out more about _____.

3. I am still confused about _____.

Team Project

Create a job application portfolio.

Part 1: By yourself, you will create a job application portfolio, which will contain all the information you need to apply for a job and go to a practice interview.

1. List all of the information you want to include in your portfolio.

2. Create the different parts of your portfolio.

- All portfolios must include the following: a resume, a cover letter, and sample interview questions and answers.
- Other items that might be included in the portfolios: certificates, awards, transcripts, performance reviews, letters of recommendation.

Create a job advertisement and conduct interviews.

Part 2: With a team, you will write a brief job advertisement and interview other students for that job.

1. Form a team with four students. Choose positions for each member of your team.

POSITION	JOB DESCRIPTION	STUDENT NAME
Student 1: **Company Owner**	See that everyone speaks English and participates.	
Student 2: **Department Supervisor**	Write job advertisement and interview questions.	
Student 3: **Company President**	Ask interview questions.	
Student 4: **Human Resources Director**	Create evaluation form.	

2. Decide what company you work for and for what position you are hiring. Write a job advertisement for the position.

3. Prepare a list of interview questions that you will ask the applicants.

4. Decide what you are looking for in an employee and create an evaluation form.

5. Once your classmates have seen all of the job advertisements and decided on a job to apply for, interview and evaluate the applicants.

6. Choose the best person for the job.

On the Job

GOALS

➤ Identify appropriate and inappropriate workplace behavior

➤ Identify workplace actions

➤ Communicate problems to a supervisor

➤ Make ethical decisions

➤ Ask for a raise

LESSON **1**

She's late, isn't she?

GOAL ➤ Identify appropriate and inappropriate workplace behavior

 Imagine that you are at work. Think carefully about each action below and decide if it is appropriate (A) or inappropriate (I) workplace behavior. Write *A* or *I* next to each statement.

_____ Ask a coworker for help.

_____ Ask for a raise.

_____ Ask your supervisor a question.

_____ Call in sick (when you are really sick).

_____ Send personal e-mails.

_____ Sit on your desk.

_____ Come back from break early.

_____ Smoke while you're working.

_____ Talk to a friend on the phone.

_____ Do Internet research for your child's school project.

_____ Take products home for your friends and family.

_____ Talk to your boss about a problem with a coworker.

_____ Arrive a few minutes late.

_____ Tell your boss you don't understand something he or she said.

 Discuss your answers with a group and think of three more examples of both appropriate and inappropriate workplace behavior. Share your ideas with the class.

GOAL ➤ **Identify appropriate and inappropriate workplace behavior**

C Compare these two questions. Which is a tag question?

"Is she late for work?"

I have no idea, but I want to know.

"She's late for work again, isn't she?"

I'm not 100% sure, but I think this is true.

D Read the questions and answers below about the tag question.

Tag question: She's late for work again, isn't she?

Q: Why is this called a tag question?
A: Because it's a question tagged onto the end of a sentence.

Q: When do we use tag questions?
A: When we are almost sure something is true, but we want to check and be 100% sure.

Q: When I'm asking a tag question, how do I know if the tag should be positive or negative?
A: If the sentence is positive, the tag is negative. If the sentence is negative, the tag is positive.

Q: What verb tense do I use in the tag?
A: Use the same verb tense in the tag that is used in the beginning of the statement.

E Study the chart with your teacher.

Tag Questions			
Positive statement	**Tag**	**Negative statement**	**Tag**
She works,	doesn't she?	She doesn't work,	does she?
She is working,	isn't she?	She isn't working,	is she?
She worked,	didn't she?	She didn't work,	did she?
She will work,	won't she?	She won't work,	will she?
She is going to work,	isn't she?	She isn't going to work,	is she?
She has worked,	hasn't she?	She hasn't worked,	has she?
She had worked,	hadn't she?	She hadn't worked,	had she?

GOAL ➤ Identify appropriate and
inappropriate workplace behavior

F Complete the questions with the correct tag.

1. He isn't e-mailing a friend, _____ ?

2. Lisa and Jack have never missed a day of work, _____ ?

3. Maria works late every night, _____ ?

4. Our coworkers will be fired next week, _____ ?

5. My assistant is going to eat lunch during the meeting, _____ ?

6. She didn't finish her work, _____ ?

7. The supervisor said to wait until tomorrow to ask for a raise, _____ ?

8. He wore shorts to his interview, _____ ?

9. Roberto had stolen things before, _____ ?

10. We'll have a business meeting next week, _____ ?

CD 1
TR 24

G Listen to the tag questions. Fill in the circle next to the tag that you hear.

1. ○ did he?   ○ didn't he?   ○ does he?   ○ doesn't he?
2. ○ won't she?   ○ will she?   ○ won't we?   ○ don't we?
3. ○ did they?   ○ did he?   ○ didn't they? ○ didn't he?
4. ○ hasn't she? ○ did she?   ○ didn't she?   ○ has she?
5. ○ are you?   ○ aren't you?   ○ isn't you?   ○ were you?

H Write three tag questions about inappropriate workplace behavior.

EXAMPLE: <u>She told her boss he looked bad, didn't she?</u>

1. _____

2. _____

3. _____

I Write three tag questions about appropriate workplace behavior.

EXAMPLE: <u>She wore a suit to the interview, didn't she?</u>

1. _____

2. _____

3. _____

The note was written by Jim.

GOAL ➤ **Identify workplace actions**

> Where are these people?
> What are they talking about?
> What can you see on the desk?

CD 1
TR 25

A **Read and listen to the conversation.**

Raquel: Did you see the note I put on your screen?

Bruno: Was that note from you? I thought it was put there by Jim.

Raquel: Actually, the note was written by Jim, but I taped it to your screen. I wanted to make sure you got it before you left for lunch.

Bruno: I did get it. The orders were sent to me yesterday, and I'll have them ready for your signature before I leave today.

Raquel: Great! I'll sign them in the morning, and then you can send them to the finance department. Make sure they are sent by Package Express.

Bruno: I'll take care of it right away.

B **Answer the questions about the conversation.**

1. Who are the two people in the conversation? Who is the supervisor?
2. What was the misunderstanding?
3. What was sent to Bruno?

C **Practice the conversation again, but this time, replace some of the words and phrases with the new words below.**

screen	→	computer
note	→	memo
lunch	→	the day
the finance department	→	human resources
right away	→	as soon as possible

D Study the chart. Compare the sentences in the passive voice with those in the active voice. What are the differences?

Passive Voice	Active Voice
The note was put there by Raquel.	Raquel put the note there.
The note was written by Jim.	Jim wrote the note.
The orders were sent yesterday. (We don't know who sent them.)	They sent the orders yesterday.

E Decide if each sentence is active (A) or passive (P). Write *A* or *P* on each line.

1. The copy machine was repaired last week. ___

2. My manager wrote the report. ___

3. The dishwashers were laid off by their supervisor. ___

4. Was the package received? ___

5. Eli designed the new brochure. ___

6. The new office building was built last year. ___

7. Our new employees were given an orientation. ___

8. Kelli was given a raise last week. ___

9. James and Brian started their own business. ___

10. José quit. ___

F Rewrite each sentence in the active voice. (*Hint:* Use the simple past tense.)

EXAMPLE: Three dishwashers were laid off by the supervisor.

    <u>The supervisor laid off three dishwashers.</u>

1. Our new employees were given an orientation by the manager.

    _____

2. Kelli was given a raise last week by the owner of the company.

    _____

3. The package was received by the receptionist.

    _____

GOAL ➤ **Identify workplace actions**

 G Study the chart below.

Passive Voice				
Example sentence	**Passive subject**	**be**	**Past participle**	**(by + person or thing)**
The note was written by Jim.	It	was	written	by Jim
The orders were sent yesterday. (We don't know who sent them.)	They	were	sent	

- Use the passive voice to emphasize the object of the action, or when the doer of the action is unknown or unimportant.
- To change an active sentence into a passive sentence, switch the subject and the object, and change the verb to the correct tense of *be* + the past participle. The word *by* is used before the doer of the action.

 H Change the sentences from active voice to passive voice.

EXAMPLE: Our delivery person brought twelve bottles of water this morning.

<u>Twelve bottles of water were brought by our delivery person this morning.</u>

1. The receptionist bought all the supplies.

_____

2. The repairperson fixed the copy machine.

_____

3. Someone stole his money and driver's license.

_____

4. A nurse took my blood pressure.

_____

I Think of three things you did at work last week. Write three passive voice sentences.

1. _____

2. _____

3. _____

LESSON 3

Taking action

GOAL ➤ Communicate problems to a supervisor

CD 1
TR 26

A Read and listen to the conversation.

Construction Worker: Excuse me, do you have a second?
Supervisor: Sure. What is it?
Construction Worker: Well, there's a small problem. The shipment of lumber didn't arrive, so we have to stop construction until it gets here. What would you like us to do?
Supervisor: There's nothing else you can do while you are waiting for it?
Construction Worker: No. We need that lumber to start working on the door frames.
Supervisor: OK. Well, why don't you guys take lunch early, and I'll call and see where the lumber is?
Construction Worker: Let me make sure I understand you correctly. You want all of us to go on lunch break right now while you call and find out where the lumber is?
Supervisor: That's right.
Construction Worker: When should we come back?
Supervisor: In about an hour.
Construction Worker: Thank you. See you in an hour.

B Answer the questions about the conversation.

1. What is the problem?
2. What does the employee say to get the supervisor's attention?
3. Does the supervisor understand the problem?
4. What does he suggest they do to solve the problem?

How to get someone's attention politely	How to check that you have understood
Excuse me, sir/ma'am/(name). Do you have a minute?	Let me make sure I understand you.
	What you are saying is . . .
Pardon me, sir/ma'am/(name). Can I talk to you for a second?	So what we/I should do is . . .

GOAL ➤ **Communicate problems to a supervisor**

C Read the flowchart. Do you agree with each step?

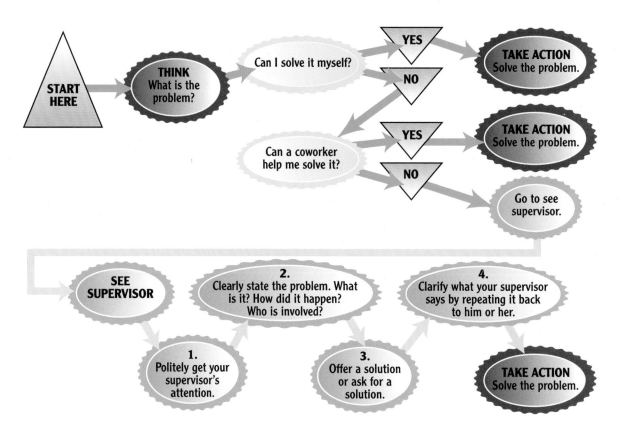

D Discuss these questions with a partner.

1. If you can solve the problem by yourself, what should you do?
2. If a coworker can help you solve the problem, what should you do?
3. When you go to see your supervisor, what is the first thing you should do? What is the last thing you should do?

How to offer a solution

Why don't we/I . . .
What if we/I . . .
Would it work if we/I . . .

E Look at the conversation on page 127. Did the construction worker follow the steps in the flowchart?

 With a group, read each situation below. Following the steps in the flowchart on page 128, discuss what you would do if you were in the situations.

1. Renee is a cashier in a fast-food restaurant. A customer just came up to the counter and told her that she gave him the wrong change. He doesn't have his receipt, and she doesn't remember helping him. What should she do?
2. Mikhail came back from lunch and found a message marked *urgent* on his desk, but it wasn't addressed to him. He doesn't recognize the name of the addressee so he doesn't know what to do with it. What should he do?
3. James and Sara assemble telephones. For this particular group of phones, they have an uneven amount of parts and aren't able to finish 20 of the phones. What should they do?

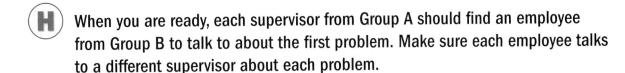 Separate your class into two groups. Read your group's directions.

Group A: **Supervisors**
As a group, discuss how you would solve each of the employees' problems below. Be prepared to communicate this to the employee when he or she asks you.

Group B: **Employees**
As a group, discuss what you would say to your supervisor about each of the problems below. Remember the four steps from the flowchart.

<u>Problems</u>
1. You just received your paycheck, and you notice that you didn't get paid for the overtime hours you worked.
2. There is an emergency phone call for you, but, if you leave your place, you will throw off the assembly line.
3. You are out installing cable TV at a customer's home, and the customer is unhappy with your service.

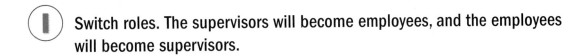 When you are ready, each supervisor from Group A should find an employee from Group B to talk to about the first problem. Make sure each employee talks to a different supervisor about each problem.

I Switch roles. The supervisors will become employees, and the employees will become supervisors.

What should you do?

GOAL ➤ **Make ethical decisions**

Vocabulary Grammar
Life Skills
Academic Pronunciation

> **ethics:** *n.* moral rules or principles of behavior
> for deciding what is right and wrong; *adj.* – **ethical**

A Each situation below describes an ethical question that you might face. What would you do? Check (✓) your answers and discuss them with a partner.

1. You pay the cashier at the supermarket with a ten-dollar bill. He gives you change as if you had given him a twenty-dollar-bill. What would you do?

    ____ Tell her. ____ Keep the extra money.

2. It's the night before the final exam at your school and you haven't had much time to study. A classmate has stolen the answers to the exam and offers to share them with you. What would you do?

    ____ Say no. ____ Borrow the answers from him.

3. You go shopping and buy some books. When you get home, you realize that the clerk put an extra book in your bag that you didn't pay for. What would you do?

    ____ Go back to the store and give the book back. ____ Keep it.

GOAL ➤ **Make ethical decisions**

Vocabulary Grammar
Life Skills
Academic Pronunciation

B In situations like the ones in Exercise A, you know what you should do, but do you always do it? Sometimes the decision is not easy, but there are steps you can take to help you make a good decision.

Steps for Making an Ethical Decision
1. Identify the ethical issue or problem.
2. List the facts that are most relevant to your decision.
3. Identify the people who might be affected by your decision and how.
4. Explain what each person would want you to do about the issue.
5. List three different decisions you could make and what the outcome of each decision would be.
6. Decide what you will do.

C Using the steps above, discuss one of the situations in Exercise A with a group and decide what would be the best thing to do.

D Read the situations below. Which one is the worst?

1. Ricardo, the night security guard, has access to all of the buildings at night. It is a slow night and he wants to check his personal e-mail using one of the available computers. The company has a strict policy about e-mail being used for business purposes only, but Ricardo is the only person in the building.

2. Emilia is a janitor who is in charge of cleaning the restrooms and refilling the supplies. She is the only one with a key to the supply closet. Her husband is very sick and she is having trouble making enough money to support her family. Often they can't afford food and they can't afford to buy toilet paper and soap.

3. Kimberly, who works as a receptionist in the front office, has access to the copy machine to make copies for other employees. Her daughter, Alyse, needs some copies for a school project. She brought her own paper and needs 200 copies for her class. She needs to have the copies or she will fail the project. The copier does not require a security code and they don't keep track of who makes how many copies.

4. Brandon works in Quality Control helping refurbish used computers. Once a year, his supervisor gives away computers to a local elementary school. He doesn't keep any record of this, and Brandon really needs a computer for his son who is just starting high school. His supervisor asks him to deliver twelve computers to a local school.

GOAL ➤ **Make ethical decisions**

E Work with a partner and choose one of the situations from Exercise D. Follow the steps for making an ethical decision in Exercise B and answer the questions below.

1. What is the ethical problem?

_____

_____

2. What are the relevant facts?

_____

_____

3. Which people are involved and how would each person be affected?

_____

_____

_____

4. What would each person want you to do?

_____

_____

_____

5. What are three different possible decisions?

_____

_____

_____

6. What is your final decision?

_____

_____

F On a separate piece of paper, write a description of an actual situation where you had to make an ethical choice. What did you do? How did you feel afterwards?

A raise

GOAL ➤ **Ask for a raise**

A Discuss these questions with your group.

1. Have you ever received a raise at your job? If yes, what was it for?
2. Have you ever asked for a raise? If yes, did you get it? If no, did your manager or supervisor explain to you why you didn't get it?

B Many people hesitate to ask for a raise. Can you think of some reasons why? List them.

_____

_____

_____

C Raj met with his boss yesterday to ask for a raise. Read about his experience.

Raj has been working for EJ Electronics as an assembler for two years. In the past year, he has come up with new ways to make the assembly line more efficient and helped increase productivity in his department. Raj thinks he deserves a raise. He has friends who work at other electronics companies, and he has been asking around to find out what different employees are paid. He believes that with his experience and his contributions to the company, his boss should give him a raise.

First, Raj went to see Heidi in Human Resources and asked her what procedures he needed to follow to ask for a raise. She suggested that he make an appointment with his boss. So, last week, he asked his boss if the two of them could sit down and have a meeting. When his boss agreed, he began to gather his paperwork: job evaluations, memos from his supervisor about the new assembly-line configurations, his "Employee of the Month" award, and records of his attendance at work. He sat down and thought about all the questions his boss might ask him and he wrote out detailed answers. Then, he asked his cousin to help him practice by asking him those questions.

D Answer the questions.

1. Do you think Raj deserves a raise? Why or why not?
2. Who did he talk to first after he decided to ask for a raise? What did she tell him?
3. What did he do to prepare for the meeting with his boss?

E Read the following article about getting a raise. Underline the advice that could be useful for you.

How to Ask for a Raise

Men are still earning more than women—lots more. According to the most recent Census Bureau data, the pay gap between men and women is 27 percent. This means that a woman earns 73 cents for every dollar a man earns. In other words, a woman works four weeks to earn as much as her male counterpart earns in three weeks.

How can women close the gap? Knock on the boss's door and ask for a raise! Getting a raise is not as difficult as it might seem. Here are ten tips to assist women in negotiating their annual raise.

1. Be a star performer. Make yourself indispensable to the company. Document your successes by saving e-mails and letters, and then compile them into a portfolio. Make sure to take this portfolio with you when you go to your boss.

2. Do some research. Know what other men and women in your field are paid.

3. Focus on your contributions to the company. While the raise is certainly important to you, do not focus on how it will help your credit card debt.

4. Be informed. Know the company's policy on raises by asking your human resources director.

5. Timing is everything. Don't ask when the office is hectic; wait until the pace has slowed down and the moment is right.

6. Do your homework. Rehearse and prepare responses to counter any objections your boss might have. Know ahead of time what the difficult questions might be and have your answers ready.

7. Rehearse. If you can, role-play the scenario with a friend or colleague. This will help you to become more comfortable when you are actually face-to-face with your boss.

8. Be professional. Ask for a formal meeting with your boss.

9. Cover your bases. Make four points about your contributions prior to asking for the raise. Illustrate your ability:
- to find solutions,
- to go above and beyond your job responsibilities,
- to help others, and, most importantly,
- to increase the company's profitability.

10. Don't take *no* for an answer. Negotiate more vacation time, stock options, 401K contribution, or flextime. Set goals and ask for another review in three months.

F Discuss these questions with a group.

1. This article focuses on how women should ask for a raise. Do you think these same ideas apply to men? Why or why not?
2. Which aspect of asking for a raise do you think is the most difficult? Take a poll among your group members.

G **Read the memo that Rogelio wrote to his supervisor asking for a raise.**

Dear Mr. Michalski,

I'm writing this letter to ask you to consider giving me raise. I have been working at Mitchel George Manufacturing for five years, and I really like my job here. I started out as a warehouse packer, and now I work in the shipping department.

I feel like I deserve a raise because, in the past year, I have been given more responsibilities on my shift. I have trained ten new employees and become a team leader. I have increased efficiency in my department by implementing a new flow system that helps us pack and ship the boxes in less time. Therefore, I hope that you will consider giving me a raise.

I would like to sit down and discuss this possibility with you as soon as it is convenient for you. Thank you for your time.

Sincerely,
Rogelio Rodriguez

H **Read the letter again and check (✓) the items Rogelio included in his letter.**

____ *thank you* to his supervisor for reading the letter

____ reason for the letter

____ how long he has been working for the company

____ what his job is

____ how his job has changed since he has been there

____ things he has done to help the company

I **You can ask for a raise in person or by writing a letter or e-mail. What are the advantages and disadvantages of each method?**

J **Let's get ready to ask for a raise! First, answer these questions. (If you are a homemaker or a student, imagine that you get paid for what you do and are asking for more money.)**

1. Do you deserve a raise? Why or why not?
2. How long have you been working at your job?
3. When was the last time you got a raise?
4. Have you been working harder or working more hours?
5. Have you been given more responsibilities?
6. Have you gotten good reviews from your supervisors?

K **Work with a partner to practice asking for a raise, or write a letter asking for a raise.**

Review

A Add tags to the statements to make tag questions. (Lesson 1)

1. She is going to ask for a promotion, _____ ?

2. We will volunteer to help them finish, _____ ?

3. Ken gets to work early every day, _____ ?

4. Her sister can't pass her drug test, _____ ?

5. They won't get that project done, on time _____ ?

6. The boss didn't talk to his employees, _____ ?

B List two examples of appropriate and inappropriate employee behavior. (Lesson 1)

Appropriate Employee Behavior:

1. _____

2. _____

Inappropriate Employee Behavior:

1. _____

2. _____

C Use the words given below to write sentences in the passive voice. You may have to add some words. (Lesson 2)

EXAMPLE: new office building / build / Lynn Street

 <u>A new office building was built on Lynn Street.</u>

1. childcare workers / give / a raise

_____

2. machines / repair / mechanics

_____

3. roses / cut / gardeners

_____

4. computer / buy / the finance department

_____

5. reports / write / two weeks ago

_____

6. package / sent / express mail

_____

D What are two ways to politely get someone's attention? Write them below. (Lesson 3)

1. _____

2. _____

E Recall what you learned about communicating a problem to a supervisor. Circle the best answer. (Lesson 3)

1. What is the first step in communicating a problem to a supervisor?
   a. Take action.
   b. Think about what the problem is.
   c. Offer a solution.

2. What should you do if you can solve the problem yourself?
   a. Take action and solve the problem yourself.
   b. Ask a coworker for help.
   c. Offer a solution.

3. What should you do if you and your coworker can't solve the problem yourselves?
   a. Take action.
   b. Think about what the problem is.
   c. Go see your supervisor.

4. What is the first thing you should do when you talk to your supervisor?
   a. Ask for a solution.
   b. Think about what the problem is.
   c. Politely get his or her attention.

5. After your supervisor offers a solution, what should you do?
   a. Ask for a solution.
   b. Clarify what your supervisor has said by repeating it back to him or her.
   c. Take action and solve the problem.

Review

F What are the six steps to making an ethical decision? List them below. (Lesson 4)

1. _____
2. _____
3. _____
4. _____
5. _____
6. _____

G Read the situation. Based on the steps you wrote above, what would you do? (Lesson 4)

> You work in a restaurant and you notice that your coworker is taking food off of the customers' plates before they are served—a French fry here, a carrot there. You know that your coworker is supporting a very large family and doesn't have enough money to feed everyone. What would you do?

_____

_____

_____

_____

H You read ten suggestions on how to ask for a raise. List them in your own words. (Lesson 5)

1. _____
2. _____
3. _____
4. _____
5. _____
6. _____
7. _____
8. _____
9. _____
10. _____

My Dictionary

Synonyms are words that have the same or similar meanings.

EXAMPLES: problem—*difficulty, hard time*
          solution—*answer, explanation*

Can you think of synonyms for these words? Use a dictionary if you need help.

fact   _____

decision   _____

rehearse   _____

illustrate   _____

contributions _____

Now look in your dictionary and see if you can add synonyms to any of your entries.

Learner Log

In this unit, you learned many things about being on the job. How comfortable do you feel doing each of the skills listed below? Rate your comfort level on a scale of 1 to 4.

1 = Need more practice   **2** = OK   **3** = Good   **4** = Great!

Life Skill	Comfort Level	Page
I can identify appropriate and inappropriate workplace behavior.	1 2 3 4	_____
I can identify workplace actions.	1 2 3 4	_____
I can communicate problems to supervisors.	1 2 3 4	_____
I can make ethical decisions.	1 2 3 4	_____
I can ask for a raise.	1 2 3 4	_____

If you circled 1 or 2, write down the page number where you can review this skill.

Reflection

1. I learned _____.

2. I would like to find out more about _____.

3. I am still confused about _____.

Team Project

Solve a company problem.

With a team, you will solve a company problem in an action committee and create a handout for the class.

1. Form a human resources action committee with four or five students. Choose positions for each member of your team.

POSITION	JOB DESCRIPTION	STUDENT NAME
Student 1: **Human Resources Director**	See that everyone speaks English and participates.	
Student 2: **Secretary**	Take notes and write information for handout.	
Student 3: **Designer**	Prepare final handout.	
Students 4/5: **Spokespeople**	Report final decision to the class.	

2. With your group, carefully read the problem below.

3. Use the steps for making an ethical decision from page 131 as you consider each possible solution.

4. Make a final decision.

5. Create a handout explaining the process you went through to come up with your decision.

6. Report your final decision to the class.

Company: RB Aerospace—Refurbishes and designs airplane interiors
Problem: A group of employees discovers that the quality of some of the parts they are using is not up to standard. They are worried that this may cause safety problems when the aircraft is in use. They have mentioned it to the quality control supervisor, but the factory is on a tight schedule and if they don't deliver this contract on time, they may lose future contracts.

Civic Responsibility

GOALS

➤ Interpret civic responsibilities
➤ Apply for a driver's license and respond to a jury summons

➤ Communicate opinions about a community problem
➤ Interpret the electoral process
➤ Write and give a speech

LESSON 1

Solving problems

GOAL ➤ Interpret civic responsibilities

Vocabulary · Grammar · Life Skills · Academic · Pronunciation

 A Why are these things important? Complete the sentences below.

jury summons	driver's license	ticket	car registration	taxes

1. A _____ permits you to drive a car.

2. _____ help pay for government programs.

3. A _____ shows that you have paid to register your car with the state.

4. A _____ indicates that you have violated a traffic law.

5. A _____ notifies you that the court needs you to appear for jury selection.

B A group of students from all over the country is attending a workshop about civic responsibility in the United States. Read their conversation and see if you can define *civic responsibility* with your teacher.

Bita: I never realized how difficult it would be to get adjusted to life in the United States. There are so many things to do.

Consuela: I know. Getting a driver's license and registering my car was very complicated.

Ranjit: In New York, we have good public transportation so I don't have to worry about a car. But I did get a jury summons the other day and I didn't know what I was supposed to do with it.

Ricardo: I got one of those last year and I couldn't understand it so I threw it away.

Minh: You threw it away? You can't do that. You have to respond.

Bita: What about tickets? The other day, I got a ticket for jaywalking. I want to fight it, but I don't know where to go.

Ranjit: I think you have to go to court, don't you?

Minh: The most confusing thing I've had to do is pay taxes. Can't they make those forms easier to understand?

Consuela: I agree. Last year, we paid someone to do our taxes.

C What five situations do the students mention?

1. getting a driver's license _____

2. _____

3. _____

4. _____

5. _____

D Can you think of other situations you have had to deal with in the United States that are related to civic responsibility? Write them on the lines below.

_____

_____

_____

E Do you have a driver's license? How did you get it? Share your experience with a group of students.

CD 1
TR 27

F Bita telephones Consuela to ask how to get a driver's license. Listen to the conversation.

G With a partner, ask and answer the questions based on what you learned from the conversation.

1. If I already have my driver's license from another country, do I still have to take the test?

2. How do I prepare for the written test?

3. How many questions are on the test?

4. How many questions do I have to get correct?

5. What if I don't pass it the first time?

6. What do I need to know about the driving test?

7. How do I apply for the license?

8. Do I need to make an appointment to turn in my application?

9. What do I have to do when I turn in my application?

10. How much does it cost?

 H In groups, ask and answer questions about situations related to the civic responsibilities that you listed on page 142.

EXAMPLE: *Student A:* Have you ever gotten a ticket before?
          Student B: Yes, I got one for rolling through a stop sign.

A driver's license and jury duty

GOAL ➤ Apply for a driver's license
and respond to a jury summons

 A Bita went to the DMV and got an application for a driver's license. Fill out the application.

DRIVER'S LICENSE APPLICATION

Name

Street/PO Box

City	State	Zip

Date of Birth	Sex ❑ Male ❑ Female	Height	Weight

License Number	Social Security No.	Restricted Code

| | Eye Color
❑ Blue ❑ Brown ❑ Black ❑ Green
❑ Gray ❑ Violet ❑ Hazel | |

Do you have any condition which might affect your ability to operate a motor vehicle, such as:

❑ Seizures or Unconsciousness	❑ Hearing or Vision Problem	❑ Have Your Driving Privileges Ever Been Suspended?
❑ Mental Disability	❑ Alcohol or Drug Problem	

***If any of the above are checked, a letter of explanation must accompany this application. Failure to do so may delay your license.

I certify that the above statements are true. Do you wish to be an organ donor? ❑ Yes ❑ No

Signed X	Date

Please check one of the following:
❑ Regular Driver's License (Class E)
❑ Out-of-State Transfer
  (Must surrender license from other state.)
❑ Applicant Under Age of 18
  *Must Provide School Enrollment Form
  *License Will Expire on 21st Birthday
	<u>DUPLICATE LICENSE FEE: $5.00</u>
	❑ Duplicate License
	❑ Duplicate Class D License
	❑ Address change: If you move, you must change your address on your driver's license within twenty days.
	❑ Name Change: _____
	
	FORMER NAME
	*You must attach a copy of your marriage certificate, divorce decree, court order or birth certificate when changing your name.

DEPARTMENT USE ONLY
Your birth certificate must be shown to the examining officer as proof of your age.
The Applicant Named in This Application Passed the Examination Conducted.
At _____ Detachment This _____ Day of _____ 20 ___

Examiner _____   Unit Number _____

Restrictions _____

 B With a group, make a chart that explains how to get a driver's license step-by-step. Compare your chart with another group's chart.

 Bita and Ranjit are chatting about jury duty in the United States. Read their conversation.

Bita: Ranjit, I just got my new driver's license in the mail!

Ranjit: Congratulations, Bita! That's wonderful.

Bita: What are you looking at?

Ranjit: Oh, I just got a jury summons in the mail. Can you tell me what I'm supposed to do with it?

Bita: Sure. I've had at least three of them.

Ranjit: What are they about anyway?

Bita: Well, in the United States, anyone accused of a crime has the right to a fair trial, which means a judge and twelve people on a jury get to listen to the case and make a decision.

Ranjit: Oh, I get it. So, can anyone be on a jury?

Bita: No, you have to meet certain qualifications.

Ranjit: Like what?

Bita: First of all, you have to be a U.S. citizen and a resident of the county or city where the trial is taking place. Also, you have to be able to understand and speak enough English to participate in the jury selection and the trial.

Ranjit: Well, I think I can speak and understand enough English, but I'm not a citizen yet. Does that disqualify me?

Bita: I'm afraid so.

Ranjit: Darn. It sounds like fun to participate in a trial. So, what do I do with this form?

Bita: There should be a series of *yes/no* questions on it. Answer each of the questions truthfully. Then explain at the bottom why you are not qualified to participate. Some people who are citizens can be excused for other reasons, like financial hardship, medical conditions, or being older than 65. So, just fill out the form and then send it back in within ten days.

Ranjit: That's it?

Bita: That's it. Easy, huh?

 Discuss the following terms with your teacher. See if you can work out their meanings using the conversation above.

fair trial	judge	accused of a crime
jury	jury selection	qualifications

GOAL ➤ **Apply for a driver's license and respond to a jury summons**

E Read the jury summons with your teacher.

JURY SUMMONS

Please bring this upper portion with you when you report for jury duty.

JUROR	You are hereby notified that you have been selected for jury service in the State Trial Courts of _____ County. You are ordered to appear at the court for the following days: *May 3, 4, 5* Your Group Number: 75 Your Juror Number: 567

JUROR QUALIFICATION FORM
DETACH THIS HALF AND RETURN BY MAIL WITHIN 10 DAYS

Name _____

Address _____

City/State/Zip _____

Home Phone _____ Date of Birth _____

Employer _____

Occupation _____

Work Phone _____

Answer each of the following questions under penalty of perjury.

1. Are you a citizen of the United States? ▢ yes ▢ no
2. Are you currently a resident of _____ County? ▢ yes ▢ no
3. Are you 18 years of age or older? ▢ yes ▢ no
4. Do you read, write, speak, and understand the English language? (If another person filled out this form, please provide their name, address, and the reasons in the space provided below.) ▢ yes ▢ no
5. Have you ever been convicted or plead guilty to theft or any felony offense? ▢ yes ▢ no
6. Do you have a physical or mental disability that would interfere with or prevent you from serving as a juror? ▢ yes ▢ no
7. Are you 65 years of age or older? ▢ yes ▢ no

If you answered NO to questions 1, 2, 3, or 4, you are automatically excused from jury duty. Please write your reason below and send in the form.

Reason I cannot serve on jury duty: _____

_____

_____

F Fill out this jury summons with your personal information. What should you do with this form when you have filled it out?

Note: If the information is too personal, just think about the answer and don't write it in your book.

Problems in your community

GOAL ➤ **Communicate opinions about a community problem**

A Look at the photos below and identify what these community problems might be.

B List the problems below. Discuss some possible solutions for each with a partner. Write one solution for each problem.

Problem	Solution
1.	
2.	
3.	
4.	

C Share your solutions with the class. Vote on the best solution for each problem.

 D Imagine you are meeting with a government official in your community. Practice the conversation below.

Official: So, what do you think one of the biggest problems in our community is?
Resident: I think the biggest problem is <u>the number of homeless people who sleep on the street</u>.
Official: Do you have any ideas about how to solve the problem?
Resident: Actually, our neighborhood came up with two ideas. One, <u>we would like to spend our tax dollars to build a bigger homeless shelter</u>. And two, <u>we would like to put a community group together to tell the homeless people about the shelter and take them there if necessary</u>.
Official: Those are two great ideas. I'll bring them up at our next town hall meeting.

E What are some problems in your community? Work with a group to make a list. Then, come up with two possible solutions for each problem.

Problem	Solution
1.	1. 2.
2.	1. 2.
3.	1. 2.

 F Work with a partner to practice the conversation in Exercise D again. This time, substitute the information you wrote in Exercise E for the underlined information.

G Prepare to write a business letter about a problem in your community. Choose one of the problems that you have discussed with your group or a different problem in your community. Before writing the letter, fill in the information below.

Date: _____

Your name and address: _____
_____

Official's name and address: (Research this information.) _____
_____

State the problem: _____
_____
_____
_____

Facts or anecdotes about the problem: _____
_____
_____
_____

Suggested solutions: _____
_____
_____

Closing: _____

H Now, write a letter to a local official about the community problem and your solution. Format it like a business letter.

GOAL ➤ Interpret the electoral process

 The students are chatting about local elections. Read their conversation. Do you agree with them? Why is it important to understand the electoral process?

Ranjit: Elections for a new mayor are coming up here in New York. Have any of you participated in an election before?

Bita: I haven't. I just became a U.S. citizen last year so I will finally get to vote in this election.

Ricardo: So, if we're not citizens, we don't need to pay attention to the elections, do we?

Bita: Oh, I disagree. Even when I wasn't a citizen, I participated in local town meetings and city council meetings.

Consuela: Why?

Bita: Because I live in this community just like everyone else and I want my voice to be heard.

Ranjit: I agree with you, Bita. I think it's important that we voice our opinions on local issues in our community. I've been listening to the candidates' speeches to see whom I would vote for. But I don't really understand how the election process works.

Bita: Let's look at the chart our teacher gave us.

B Read the flowchart and discuss it with your classmates and teacher.

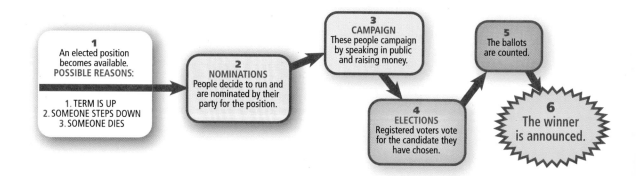

C Work with a partner. One of you should explain the words in the box below. The other partner should then explain the electoral process using these words. Switch roles when you have finished.

> elected   position   to step down   term   ballots   to announce

 Circle the best answer to each question about the electoral process.

1. When does an elected position become available?
   a. when someone's term is up
   b. when someone steps down
   c. when someone dies
   d. all of the above

2. Who nominates people to run for office?
   a. their friends and family
   b. their political party
   c. their teachers
   d. the previous elected official

3. What does it mean to campaign?
   a. vote
   b. make posters
   c. speak in public and raise money
   d. count the ballots

4. When is the winner announced?
   a. before the elections
   b. after the nominations
   c. after someone dies
   d. when all the ballots have been counted

E Are you eligible to vote in an election? Read the list of requirements and check (✓) the ones that apply to you.

Requirements	
U.S. citizen	❑ I am a U.S. citizen.
Resident of the state you live in	❑ I am a resident.
A person who is 18 years or older	❑ I am 18 years or older.
A person who is not in jail or on parole	❑ I am not in jail or on parole.

F If you checked all of the boxes in Exercise E, you are eligible to vote! What's the next step? You need to fill out a voter registration card. You can register to vote at these locations: a post office, a public library, the Department of Motor Vehicles (DMV), and other government offices.

G Fill out the voter registration card.

Official Voter Registration Card

1. NAME _____

2. RESIDENCE _____

3. MAILING ADDRESS (if different from residence) _____

4. TELEPHONE NUMBER (_____) _____-_____

5. DATE OF BIRTH ____/____/_____

6. BIRTHPLACE _____

7. OCCUPATION _____

8. PRIOR REGISTRATION _____

9. POLITICAL PARTY (CHECK ONE)

❏ American Independent Party   ❏ Democratic Party   ❏ Libertarian Party

❏ Peace And Freedom Party   ❏ Republican Party   ❏ Decline To State

Other (Specify) _____

READ THIS STATEMENT BEFORE SIGNING:
I am a citizen of the United States and will be at least 18 years of age at the time of the next election. I am not imprisoned or on parole for the conviction of a felony. I certify under penalty of perjury under the laws of the state of California that the information on this affidavit is true and correct.

_____

Signature   Date

H Write a paragraph about the electoral process. Use some of these sequencing transitions in your paragraph.

After that,	In conclusion,	First of all,
At the next stage,	In summary,	Secondly,
Next,	Finally,	Thirdly,

What's your platform?

GOAL ➤ Write and give a speech

CD 1
TR 28

A Listen to the speeches from three people running for mayor of your city. For the first speech, put a check mark (✓) next to everything the candidate promises to do for you. For the second two speeches, write down what they promise to do for you. You will hear each speech two times.

Antonio Juliana promises to:

❏ clean up the streets

❏ lower tuition fees

❏ improve public transportation

❏ decrease gang violence

❏ get kids off the streets

❏ help the homeless people

❏ increase environmental awareness

Antonio Juliana

Gary Hurt promises to:

1. clean up the beaches

2. _____

3. _____

Gary Hurt

Kwan Tan promises to:

1. _____

2. _____

3. _____

4. _____

Kwan Tan

B Who would you vote for if you were interested in . . .

the environment? _____

education? _____

safe streets? _____

C Read Kwan Tan's speech.

Good evening and thank you for coming tonight! This community has given me so many opportunities and, in running for mayor, I hope to give something back to the city that welcomed me as an immigrant, educated me through my teen years, and supported me as I opened my first business.

First on my agenda is education. I will make sure your tax dollars are used to build more schools so our children won't have to sit in overcrowded classrooms. I'll lower the tuition at our community colleges so all of us will have a chance to continue and improve our education. I'll implement standards to ensure that schools are teaching our kids what they need to know. I'll start a parent-involvement program that encourages parents to participate actively in their kids' schools. Our children are the future of our community and we should invest time and money in their success.

Vote for me on Election Day and you'll have schools and a community to be proud of!

Kwan Tan for Mayor

Kwan Tan is:
★ A local business owner
★ A member of this community for over 25 years
★ A parent of two school-age children

A vote for Kwan will ensure for our community:
★ More primary and secondary schools
★ Improved standards of education
★ More parent involvement in schools
★ Lower community college tuition

★ **Vote for Kwan Tan** ★

D What changes would Kwan like to make? Do you think these are good ideas? Discuss your opinions with a partner.

E Study the chart with your teacher.

Passive Modals				
Example sentence	**Passive subject**	**Modal**	***be***	**Past participle**
More schools *should be* built.	schools	should	be	built
Taxes *need to be* increased.	taxes	need to	be	increased
Children *must be* protected.	children	must	be	protected
Parents *have to be* involved.	parents	have to	be	involved

GOAL ➤ **Write and give a speech**

F Write sentences to describe the issues Kwan Tan wants to change.

EXAMPLE: Kwan Tan wants to build more schools.

She thinks that <u>more schools should be built</u>_____.

1. Kwan Tan wants to lower tuition fees at community colleges.

   She says that _____.

2. Kwan Tan wants to implement standards in schools.

   She thinks that _____.

3. Kwan Tan wants to encourage parents to participate in their kids' schools.

   She believes that _____.

4. Kwan Tan wants to invest time and money in children.

   She emphasizes that _____.

G Think of three problems that you would like to solve in your community. Write sentences about them using passive modals.

1. _____

2. _____

3. _____

H Kwan Tan's election speech has three parts. Look for each part in her speech.

Introduction: She introduces herself and explains why she is running for office.

Body: She tells her audience what she plans to do if she is elected.

Conclusion: She reminds her audience to vote and tells them once again what changes she will make to the community.

I Imagine that you are running for mayor of your community. How would you introduce yourself? What problems would you like to solve? Write a speech that you would give if you were running for mayor. Practice it a few times alone and then give your speech to the class.

Review

A Without looking back in the unit, try to recall what you learned about each of these topics. Write notes. (Lessons 1–5)

Topic	I learned. . .
a jury summons	
a driver's license	
the electoral process	
voting	
giving a speech	

B Are the statements below true or false? (Lessons 1–5)

	True	False
1. You have to be 18 to apply for a driver's license.	○	○
2. You must respond to a jury summons.	○	○
3. You have to be a U.S. citizen to serve on a jury.	○	○
4. You don't have to speak English to serve on a jury trial.	○	○
5. People who want to run for office must be nominated.	○	○
6. Anyone who lives in the United States can vote.	○	○
7. You can register to vote at the DMV.	○	○
8. Only U.S. citizens can get involved in the community.	○	○

C What are three problems in your community that you would like to solve? How would you solve them? Work with a small group to fill in the chart. (Lesson 3)

Problem	Solution
1.	
2.	
3.	

D There are six steps in the electoral process. Number them in the correct order. (Lesson 4)

___ Ballots are counted.

___ Elections are held.

___ Candidates campaign.

___ Candidates are nominated.

___ The winner is announced.

___ A position becomes available.

E What are the four requirements to be eligible to vote? List them below. (Lesson 4)

1. _____

2. _____

3. _____

4. _____

F What are three places where you can register to vote? List them below. (Lesson 4)

1. _____

2. _____

3. _____

G Rewrite each sentence using a passive modal. (Lesson 5)

1. We must protect the environment.

_____

2. They should reduce our taxes.

_____

3. They need to invest money in our education system.

_____

4. We have to reduce the speed limit.

_____

5. They need to build more public transportation.

_____

6. We should protect our children from gang violence.

_____

H Imagine that you are running for mayor. What are your solutions for the following problems? (Lesson 5)

1. Problem: gang violence

   Solution: _____

   _____

2. Problem: traffic

   Solution: _____

   _____

3. Problem: residents not using public transportation

   Solution: _____

   _____

4. Problem: homeless children

   Solution: _____

   _____

My Dictionary

In the past seven units, you have learned many new ways to keep track of new vocabulary. Go back through your book and make a list of all the vocabulary strategies you learned.

Vocabulary Strategies I Have Learned

Check (✓) the strategies that are most useful to you.

Learner Log

In this unit, you learned many things about civic responsibility. How comfortable do you feel doing each of the skills listed below? Rate your comfort level on a scale of 1 to 4.

1 = Need more practice   **2** = OK   **3** = Good   **4** = Great!

Life Skill	Comfort Level	Page
I can identify civic responsibilities.	1 2 3 4	_____
I can apply for a driver's license.	1 2 3 4	_____
I can respond to a jury summons.	1 2 3 4	_____
I can identify community problems and solutions.	1 2 3 4	_____
I can communicate opinions about community issues.	1 2 3 4	_____
I can write a letter to a local official.	1 2 3 4	_____
I can interpret and explain the electoral process.	1 2 3 4	_____
I can write and give a speech.	1 2 3 4	_____

If you circled 1 or 2, write down the page number where you can review this skill.

Reflections

1. I learned _____.

2. I would like to find out more about _____.

Conduct an election.

With a team, you will prepare a candidate for an election. As a class, you will conduct an election.

1. Form a campaign committee with four or five students. Choose positions for each member of your team.

POSITION	JOB DESCRIPTION	STUDENT NAME
Student 1: **Campaign Director**	See that everyone speaks English and participates.	
Student 2: **Speech Writer**	Write candidate's speech.	
Student 3: **Candidate**	Give speech to class.	
Students 4/5: **Spokespeople**	Announce nomination. Introduce candidate. Create ballot.	

2. With your group, decide who will be running for school president. Announce the nomination to the class.

3. As a class, create a ballot with all the nominees' names on it. Make a ballot box for students to put their ballots in after they vote.

4. With your group, decide what issues are most important and write a campaign speech.

5. Candidates give speeches to the class.

6. Students all vote.

7. The teacher counts the ballots and announces the winner.

Pre-Unit
achievable P7
achieved P1
adjective P7
admission application P1
adverb P7
bar graph P6
conclusion sentence P8
creation P7
decide P7
educational P7
goal P1
interview P5
maiden name P1
meet P2
native speakers P4
noun P7
organization P7
paragraph P8
strategy P5
success P7
support sentence P8
topic sentence P8
verb P7
word family P7

Unit 1
accomplish 14
achievements 14
adjective clause 11
advice 8
allocate 14
architect 4
brainstorm 7
calm 10
carpool 7
cluster diagram 7
context 4
daily journal 10
daycare facility 8
deadlines 14
designed 4
determination 12
dreams 4
firm 4
focus 10
goals 4
habits 3
hopeful 10
in advance 13
influence 10
intern 5

jewelry 4
last-minute changes 13
medicine 4
obstacle 7
organized 13
overcome 7
partner 5
patience 12
perspective 10
positive influence 12
prioritize 14
qualifications 4
raise 4
realistic 14
reality 4
refugee 4
reliable 7
respond 8
retired 4
sacrificing 14
simultaneously 14
solution 7
suburban 4
surgeon 4
task 15
time management 13
toddler 8
to the last minute 13
troubled 10
used to 2
veranda 10

Unit 2
address 35
annual fee 27
APR 27
attractive 30
bargain 24
body 35
budget 22
budgeted amount 22
capacity 27
character 27
closing 35
collateral 27
complain 33
complaint 35
credit card 27
credit limit 27
creditworthiness 27
debit card 27
delivery time 24

digital camcorder 30
digital zoom 30
down payment 29
finance 21
grace period 27
greeting 35
image 30
introductory rate 27
late fee 27
LCD 30
loan 29
miniDV 30
miniDVD 30
monthly expenses 21
optical zoom 30
personal finances 21
persuade 30
price-matching 24
return address 35
salutation 35
shipping costs 24
shop around 24
signature 35
stabilization 30
still mode 30
trust 31
utilities 21
viewfinder 30
warranty 24

Unit 3
advantages 44
afford 53
amenities 41
asking price 41
attached garage 47
brand-new 41
central heating 50
closet space 50
closing 52
comparative 46
cozy 41
credit check 53
deposit 53
detached 41
disadvantages 44
enclosed 50
essential 50
expensive taste 45
financial commitment 53
floor plan 45
get approved for a loan 53

ideal 47
location 42
make an offer 51
market 41
master suite 41
mortgage 53
needs loving care 41
negotiate 41
nightlife 41
noisy 44
offer 41
on the way 47
outgrown 47
pay stubs 53
pile into 47
preferences 47
price range 48
priority 50
purchase price 53
putting away 47
realtor 47
seasonal views 41
secluded 41
single-family 41
superlative 46
survive 47
thought long and hard 47
within walking distance 47
working fireplace 41
works out of the home 47

Unit 4
airport 70
annunciation 66
Bingo 68
bulletin board 68
campground 70
clarification 72
community organizations 73
dress code 66
flyers 69
freeway 70
interstate 70
keep track of 74
local hangout 67
locate 61
map scale 70
marathon 68
notices 68
recycling 63
reservations 66
resources 61

rest area 70
scenic 70
sign up 61
structures 74
suggestion 68
volunteer 73

Unit 5
ache 84
advise 95
allergy 95
announce 89
arthritis 95
asthma 95
calculate 83
calories 90
cancer 95
carbohydrates 90
chiropractor 88
cholesterol 87
circulatory 95
colon 95
common cold 84
co-pay 93
cough 84
coverage 93
deductible 93
dentist 88
dependants 94
diabetes 95
digestive system 95
emotional 95
examine 86
fat 90
fiber 90
flu 84
health care professional 89
healthy 81
hernia 95
high blood pressure 95
ingredients 90
intestinal 95
joint 95
junk food 87
kidney 95

liver 95
meditating 82
mental 95
mental health 82
muscle spasm 84
muscular 95
nutrients 91
obstetrician 88
optometrist 85
overweight 91
physical health 82
pediatrician 88
percentage 83
physical health 82
podiatrist 88
poll 83
premium 93
prescription plan 93
protein 90
providers 93
puzzles 82
reproductive organs 95
reputation 93
respiratory 95
saturated fat 90
serving size 90
sodium 90
spouse 94
stroke 95
throwing up 84
thyroid 95
ulcer 95
unhealthy 81
vitamins 90

Unit 6
appearance 114
appropriateness 114
benefit (v) 113
benefits (n) 104
certificate 107
characteristics 102
conflict 113
cover letter 110
criteria 115

degree 108
effectiveness 114
eye contact 114
facial expressions 114
identify 110
impression 115
interests 103
job responsibilities 102
job titles 102
key strengths 110
mock 115
overtime 104
posture 114
required qualifications 104
resume 108
self-confidence 114
skill 101
strength 113
troubleshooting 107
voice level 114
weakness 113
willingness 114

Unit 7
active 125
appropriate 121
brochure 125
Census Bureau data 134
close the gap 134
construction 127
contributions to the
  company 134
counterpart 134
cover your bases 134
deserve 135
document 134
door frames 127
ethical 130
ethics 130
flowchart 128
get someone's attention 127
hesitate 133
inappropriate 121
lumber 127
misunderstanding 124

pardon me 127
passive 125
politely 127
raise 134
rehearse 134
relevant 131
review 134
shipment 127
solution 128
star performer 134
tag 122

Unit 8
accused of a crime 145
anecdotes 149
announce 150
ballots 150
campaign 150
car registration 141
case 145
civic responsibility 141
disqualify 145
elected 150
eligible 151
environmental awareness 153
fair trial 145
gang violence 153
homeless 153
homeless shelter 148
jaywalking 142
judge 145
jury 145
jury selection 145
jury summons 141
local official 149
mental disability 146
overcrowded freeway 147
position 150
public transportation 142
qualifications 145
step down 150
taxes 141
term 150
ticket 141
tuition 153

Stand Out 4 Irregular Verb List

The following verbs are used in *Stand Out 4* and have irregular past tense forms.

Base Form	Simple Past	Past Participle
be	was, were	been
become	became	become
begin	began	begun
break	broke	broken
bring	brought	brought
build	built	built
buy	bought	bought
catch	caught	caught
come	came	come
do	did	done
drink	drank	drunk
drive	drove	driven
eat	ate	eaten
fall	fell	fallen
feel	felt	felt
fight	fought	fought
find	found	found
fly	flew	flown
get	got	gotten
give	gave	given
go	went	gone
grow	grew	grown
have	had	had
hear	heard	heard
hold	held	held
hurt	hurt	hurt
keep	kept	kept
know	knew	known
learn	learned	learned/learnt
lend	lent	lent

Base Form	Simple Past	Past Participle
lose	lost	lost
make	made	made
mean	meant	meant
meet	met	met
pay	paid	paid
put	put	put
read	read	read
ride	rode	ridden
run	ran	run
say	said	said
sell	sold	sold
send	sent	sent
set	set	set
show	showed	showed/shown
sit	sat	sat
sleep	slept	slept
speak	spoke	spoken
spend	spent	spent
spread	spread	spread
stand	stood	stood
steal	stole	stolen
take	took	taken
teach	taught	taught
tell	told	told
think	thought	thought
throw	threw	thrown
wake	woke	woken
wear	wore	worn
win	won	won
write	wrote	written

Used to

Example	Rule
Minh *used to* go to school during the day. Bita *used to* be an architect in Iran.	**Affirmative:** *used to* + base verb
Bita *did not use to* go to school at night. Minh *didn't use to* take care of his grandchildren.	**Negative:** *did* + *not* (*didn't*) + *use to* + base verb **Incorrect:** ~~I didn't used to go to school.~~
Did Minh *use to* work? *Did* Bita *use to* study English?	**Yes/No Question:** *did* + subject + *use to* + base verb **Incorrect:** ~~Did Bita used to live in Iran?~~
Where *did* Minh *use to* work? What *did* Bita *use to* study?	**Wh- Question:** *wh-* word + *did* + subject + *use to* + base verb

Used to + base verb expresses a past habit or state which is now different.

Future Tense Using *Will*

Example	Rule
In the spring of 2009, *I will ask* my boss for a raise. In the summer, *I will look* for a job.	Future tense = *will* + base verb

In spoken English, people often use contractions: I will = *I'll*.

Adjective Clauses

Main clause (Subject clause)	Relative pronoun	Adjective clause
This is the place	where	I grew up.
She is the person	who (that)	influenced me most.
A journal is something	which (that)	can help you focus on important things.
Main clause (Object clause)	**Relative pronoun**	**Adjective clause**
This is the woman	who (whom)	I met yesterday.
Here is the book	which	you gave me this morning.

Adjectival clauses describe a preceding noun. They can describe a subject noun or an object noun.
If the noun is an object, you can leave out the relative pronoun.

Contrary-to-Fact Conditionals

Condition (*if* + past tense verb)	Result (*would* + base verb)
If she *got* a raise,	she *would buy* a new house.
If they *didn't spend* so much money on rent,	they *would have* more money for entertainment.
If I *were* a millionaire,	I *would give* all my money to charity.
If John *weren't* so busy at work,	he *would spend* more time with his children.

- *Contrary-to-fact* (or *unreal*) *conditional statements* are sentences that are not true.
- The *if*-clause can come in the first or second part of the sentence. Notice how commas are used in the examples. (If you reverse the order of the condition and result clauses, omit the comma.)
- In written English, use *were* (instead of *was*) for *if*-clauses with first and third person singular forms of *be*.
- In spoken English, people often use contractions: I would = *I'd*; she would = *she'd*, etc.

Contrary-to-Fact Questions

Wh-Question	*Yes/No* Question
What + *would* + subject + base verb + *if* + subject + past tense	*Would* + subject + base verb + *if* + subject + past tense
What would you do *if* you won the lottery?	*Would* you give up your job *if* you won the lottery?

Passive Voice: Present Tense

Subject	*be*	Past Participle		Explanation
Ads	are	written	to sell products.	Since we know that ads are written by advertisers, the information "by advertisers" is not important.
The camera	is	advertised	on television.	Since we know that the store is advertising the camera, the information "by the store" is not important.

We use the passive voice to emphasize the object of the action or when the doer is not important.

Questions Using Comparative and Superlative Adjectives

Question word	Subject	Verb	Adjective or Noun	Rule
Which	one place house	is	bigger? closer to work? the safest?	Use *be* when following the verb with an adjective.
		has	more rooms? the biggest floor plan?	Use *have* before a noun.

Long and Short Answers

Question	Short answer	Long answer	Rules
Which one is bigger, the condominium or the house?	The condominium.	The condominium is bigger. The condominium is bigger than the house.	• When talking about two things and mentioning both of them, use *than*.
Which place has more rooms?	The house.	The house has more rooms. The house has more rooms than the condominium.	• When talking about two things, but only mentioning one of them, do not use *than*.

Yes/No Questions and Answers

Do you want	air-conditioning? a backyard?	Yes, I do. No, I don't.
Do they need	a balcony? a garage?	Yes, they do. No, they don't.
Does the house have	heating? a pool?	Yes, it does. No, it doesn't.

Information Questions

Information	Example questions		
type of property	What type	of property	do you want? is it?
number of bathrooms number of bedrooms	How many	bedrooms bathrooms	do you want? does it have?
location	Where		is it?
price range	What		is your price range?
down payment (percentage)	How much		can you put down?

Embedded Questions

Introductory question	Embedded question	Rules
Can you show me	where *Orange Avenue is*?	In an embedded information question, the subject comes before the verb.
Do you know	if there is a library near here?	For *yes/no* questions, use *if* before the embedded question.
Can you tell me	when the library opens?	For questions with *do* or *does*, take out *do/does* and use the base form of the verb.

Why do we use embedded questions? They sound more polite than direct questions.

Present Perfect Continuous

Example	Form
I *have been resting* for three hours.	*Affirmative sentence*: has/have + been + present participle
He *hasn't been sleeping* well recently.	*Negative sentence*: has/have + not + been + present participle
How *long have they lived/have they been living* here?	*Question*: has/have + subject + been + present participle

- To emphasize the duration of an activity or state that started in the past and continues in the present. Example: The president *has been sleeping* since 9 A.M.
- To show that an activity has been in progress recently. Example: You've *been going* to the doctor a lot lately.
- With some verbs (*work, live, teach*), there is no difference in meaning between the present perfect simple and the present perfect continuous. Example: They *have lived/have been living* here since 2000.

Note: Some verbs are not usually used in the continuous form. These include *be, believe, hate, have, know, like,* and *want.*

Present Perfect Simple

Example	Form
He *has seen* the doctor. I *have moved* four times in my life.	*Affirmative sentence*: has/have + past participle
They *haven't been* to the hospital to see her.	*Negative sentence*: has/have + not + past participle OR has/have + never + past participle
Have you *written* to your mother?	*Question*: has/have + subject + past participle

- When something happened (or didn't happen) at an unspecified time in the past. Example: She *has* never *broken* her arm.
- When something happened more than once in the past (and could possibly happen again in the future). Example: I *have moved* four times in my life.
- When something started at a specific time in the past and continues in the present. Example: They *have lived* here for ten years.

Direct Speech	Indirect Speech	Rule
"You have to exercise more."	The doctor *explained* (that) I had to exercise more.	• Change pronoun. • Change present tense to past tense.
"The most important thing is your health."	The doctor *said* (that) the most important thing was my health.	

Direct Speech	Indirect Speech
I want to lose weight.	I told *you* (that) I wanted to lose weight.
My test results are negative.	He notified *me* (that) my test results were negative.
It is important to check your heart rate.	My personal trainer said (that) it was important to check my heart rate.
I feel sick.	She complained (that) she felt sick.

- Some verbs are usually followed by an indirect object or pronoun. (*tell, assure, advise, convince, notify, promise, remind, teach, warn*)
- Some verbs are NOT followed by an indirect object or pronoun. (*say, agree, announce, answer, complain, explain, reply, state*)

Tag Questions

Positive statement	Tag	Negative statement	Tag
She works,	doesn't she?	She doesn't work,	does she?
She is working,	isn't she?	She isn't working,	is she?
She worked,	didn't she?	She didn't work,	did she?
She will work,	won't she?	She won't work,	will she?
She is going to work,	isn't she?	She isn't going to work,	is she?
She has worked,	hasn't she?	She hasn't worked,	has she?
She had worked,	hadn't she?	She hadn't worked,	had she?

Passive Voice

Example sentence	Passive subject	*be*	Past participle	(*by* + person or thing)
The note was written by Jim.	It	was	written	by Jim
The orders were sent yesterday. (We don't know who sent them.)	They	were	sent	

- Use the passive voice to emphasize the object of the action, or when the doer of the action is unknown or unimportant.
- To change an active sentence into a passive sentence, switch the subject and the object, and change the verb to the correct tense of *be* + the past participle. The word *by* is used before the doer of the action.

Passive Modals

Example sentence	Passive subject	Modal	*be*	Past participle
More schools *should be* built.	schools	should	be	built
Taxes *need to be* increased.	taxes	need to	be	increased
Children *must be* protected.	children	must	be	protected
Parents *have to be* involved.	parents	have to	be	involved

Stand Out 4 Listening Scripts

PRE-UNIT
CD 1, Track 1, Page P2
B. Read the conversation. Then, listen to the conversation.
Bita: Hi. My name is Bita. What's your name?
Minh: I'm Minh. Nice to meet you.
Bita: Where are you from, Minh?
Minh: I'm from Vietnam. And you?
Bita: I'm from Iran.
Minh: Interesting. I've never been to Iran. Tell me something about yourself.
Bita: Well, I'm studying English because I want to be an architect in the United States.
Minh: Wow! That's ambitious. Good for you!
Bita: And tell me something about yourself, Minh.
Minh: In my free time, I make jewelry and sell it to help raise money for my grandchildren to go to college.
Bita: That's wonderful! I'd love to see your jewelry sometime.
Minh: I'd be more than happy to show it to you.

UNIT 1
CD 1, Track 2, Page 1
A. Bita and Minh are new students at Bellingham Adult School. Listen to their conversation on the first day of class.
Bita: Excuse me. Is this Ms. Johnson's ESL class? I'm new here.
Minh: I'm pretty sure this is her class. I attended classes at this school five years ago, and this is where her class was.
Bita: Oh good. I used to go to school in the daytime before I got a new job. Now that I'm working during the day, I have to go to school in the evening. My other school doesn't offer evening classes so I had to leave there and come here.
Minh: I used to go to school during the day too, but sometimes I take care of my grandchildren so evening classes are better for me. What kind of work do you do?
Bita: I used to be an architect in Iran, but I don't have the right qualifications to be an architect in the United States. So, I'm doing administrative work for an engineering company until my English is good enough to go back to college and get the right degree.
Minh: Wow, I'm impressed.
Bita: Do you work?
Minh: Not anymore. I used to work for a computer company, assembling computers, but now I just go to school and help my children with their children.
Bita: That's nice. I bet your children appreciate that. Why are you studying English?
Minh: First of all, I want to help my grandchildren with their homework. But, also, I figure since I live in this country, I should be able to speak the language. Don't you agree?
Bita: Completely!

CD 1, Track 3, Page 1
C. Bita and Minh both talk about things they did in the past and things they do now. Listen again and complete the chart.
Bita: Excuse me. Is this Ms. Johnson's ESL class? I'm new here.
Minh: I'm pretty sure this is her class. I attended classes at this school five years ago, and this is where her class was.
Bita: Oh good. I used to go to school in the daytime before I got a new job. Now that I'm working during the day, I have to go to school in the evening. My other school doesn't offer evening classes so I had to leave there and come here.
Minh: I used to go to school during the day too, but sometimes I take care of my grandchildren so evening classes are better for me. What kind of work do you do?
Bita: I used to be an architect in Iran, but I don't have the right qualifications to be an architect in the United States. So, I'm doing administrative work for an engineering company until my English is good enough to go back to college and get the right degree.
Minh: Wow, I'm impressed.
Bita: Do you work?
Minh: Not anymore. I used to work for a computer company, assembling computers, but now I just go to school and help my children with their children.
Bita: That's nice. I bet your children appreciate that. Why are you studying English?
Minh: First of all, I want to help my grandchildren with their homework. But, also, I figure since I live in this country, I should be able to speak the language. Don't you agree?
Bita: Completely!

CD 1, Track 4, Page 5
F. Listen to the conversation that Bita is having with her friend, Yoshiko. Fill in Bita's goal chart with the missing steps and dates.
Yoshiko: How long do you think it will take you to become an architect?
Bita: My goal is to become a partner in a firm by the year 2017.
Yoshiko: What'll you do first?
Bita: Well, the first thing I have to do is improve my English, which I plan to study for two more years. Then by the fall of 2011, I'll be ready to register for college.

Yoshiko: How long will it take you to finish?

Bita: Well, usually a degree in architecture takes five or six years to complete, but some of the classes I took in my country will transfer, so I should be able to do it faster. I plan to get my degree in the spring of 2015.

Yoshiko: Then you can become an architect?

Bita: Not quite. Then I'll have to become an intern to get some practical experience and prepare for my licensing exams.

Yoshiko: Exams?

Bita: Yes, I'll have to take a series of tests before I can get my license to be an architect. Once I have my license, which I hope to get in the winter of 2016, I can apply to work as a partner in an architectural firm.

Yoshiko: Whew! That sounds like a lot of work!

Bita: It will be, but it'll be worth it in the end.

CD 1, Track 5, Page 8

C. Listen to each person talk to his or her friend about their problems. After you listen to each conversation, write the problem and two pieces of advice that the person receives.

Conversation 1

Anna: How's Harry doing these days?

Miyuki: I don't know what to do about him. He can't seem to settle down. He's angry all the time and is always fighting with the other students. My husband has to go and talk to the principal almost every week.

Anna: How about talking to the guidance counselor?

Miyuki: I've tried that, but he doesn't have any suggestions.

Anna: Why don't you go and observe some classes and get to know the teachers better? Maybe that would help.

Miyuki: Yes, that's a great idea.

Conversation 2

Ron: What am I going to do? My new landlord doesn't like dogs and he wants me to get rid of Herbie!

Mike: You can't do that! Has he met Herbie? Does he know what a friendly dog he is? Did you try introducing them?

Ron: No, that won't work. I don't think my landlord likes any dogs.-

Mike: OK, then why don't you start looking for another apartment?

Conversation 3

Sue: How's your back these days, Patty?

Patty: It's getting worse. I'm going to need an operation, but I don't have any insurance.

Sue: I guess you'll have to save up some money then.

Patty: Yes, it could be expensive.

Sue: Or, how about finding a job that gives you health insurance?

Patty: Yes, that's what I'll have to do.

CD 1, Track 6, Page 10

A. Look at the photos and listen to Eliana talk about why they are important to her. Then read the paragraphs.

This is a picture of the house where I grew up in Argentina. It's very important to me because it holds a lot of memories. This is the garden where I played with my brothers and sisters, and the veranda where I often sat with my parents in the evenings, listening to their stories and watching the stars and dreaming about my future.

This is the person who influenced me the most when I was young. She was my teacher in the first grade and we stayed friends until I left home. She was always so calm and gave me good advice. She was the kind of person who is able to give you another perspective on a problem and make you feel hopeful, no matter how troubled you are.

This is my daily journal. I use it to write about my feelings and hopes. It helps me understand them better. Sometimes I just write about things which happened to me during the day. My journal is something which helps me focus on the important things in my life.

UNIT 2
CD 1, Track 7, Page 21

B. Listen to Sara and Todd Mason talk about their finances. Fill in the missing numbers.

Todd: I think it's time we sat down and made a family budget. As the kids grow older, we're going to need to budget our money more wisely.

Sara: Good idea. How should we start?

Todd: Well, let's make a list of everything we spend money on, and then let's guess at how much we spend in each category. Then we'll save our receipts for next month and see how much we actually spent.

Sara: OK, why don't we start with the cars? Since both of them are paid off, we don't have any loan payments, but we do have to pay for gas, insurance, and maintenance. I'd say we spend $300 a month on gas, $150 a month on insurance, and I don't know about maintenance, but it might come to $550 a month for everything.

Todd: That sounds right. Now let's talk about rent. We know it's going to be $1,500.

Sara: Right. In the utilities category, I'd say we spend about $40 on gas, $100 on electricity, and $20 on water. That adds up to $160.

Todd: Don't forget cable, phone, and Internet. Cable is $50, phone is $95, and Internet is $45. That's $190 right there.

Sara: Wow, we spend money on a lot of things!

Todd: And we're not even finished! How much do you think we spend on food each month?

Sara: I spend about $400 a month on groceries, and I'd say we spend about $200 going out to dinner.

Todd: What about school supplies and clothing?

Sara: School supplies are about $60 a month and clothing about $200.

Todd: Are we forgetting anything? . . . Oh, medical expenses. It's a good thing we have insurance, but it doesn't pay for everything. I'd say we spend about $50 a month.

Sara: That sounds about right. And don't forget entertainment. Movies and taking the kids on trips adds up! I'd be willing to bet we spend at least $150 a month on those kinds of things—I'm afraid to add all this up!

CD 1, Track 8, Page 22

E. Now listen to Sara and Todd talk about what they actually spent in the month of May. Write their actual expenses in the third column.

Sara: I can't believe it's been a month since we sat down and wrote our budget. Time flies!

Todd: Yep, it sure does. OK, since we've already totaled up the receipts, let's write down the total amount of money we spent last month in each category.

Sara: OK, I've got the auto expenses. We spent $295.50 on gas, $150 on insurance, and nothing on maintenance. So, that's $445.50 total. That's less than what we thought.

Todd: OK, rent and utilities. Obviously, rent is what we thought—$1,500. Gas was $35.76, electricity was $150.02, and water was $22.34. That comes to $208.12. We were close on gas and water, but we were way off on the electricity.

Sara: I guess we're not used to that rate increase yet.

Todd: I don't think I'll ever get used to it. OK, cable was $50, phone was $155.72, and Internet was $30. That adds up to $235.72.

Sara: Not bad. I guess the bigger phone bill was because of all those calls you made to your mother last month. Maybe we can make her pay for it!

Todd: Oh, she'd love that! OK, what else?

Sara: I spent $359.81 last month on groceries, and we spent about $300 going out to dinner. I guess we underestimated on that one.

Todd: What about school supplies and clothing?

Sara: School supplies were about $30 and clothing was $102.14, but I still think we should leave the clothing budget at $200. The boys are still growing and they need new clothes quite often.

Todd: Good idea. We spent $45.28 on medical expenses and $132.96 on entertainment.

Sara: All right. Let's add it up!

UNIT 3
CD 1, Track 9, Page 43

E. Listen to the advertisements of homes for sale and fill in the information you hear.

1. Wanna live like a king? Then you can't pass up the Prince's Palace. Offered at a mere $1.2 million, this sprawling 15,000-square-foot palace is located at the top of a hill far away from other residences. Not only does it have every appliance you can think of, but all the rooms have beautiful hardwood floors. Wanna find out more about this princely estate? Call today!

2. Always wanted to take a house and make it your own? Here's your chance! Settle into this four-bedroom, 2,000-square-foot fixer-upper for only $150,000. Located in a busy neighborhood with lots of other families. This place is perfect for a young family.

3. Move out of the slow life and into the fast lane! A beautifully spacious 1,000-square-foot studio apartment at the top of one of the city's newest high rises is just what you're looking for. The building has 24-hour security. Utility room with washers and dryers is in the basement. The owner wants to lease it for $2,000 a month, but is willing to sell. Hurry! This one will go fast!

4. You've finally decided it's time to move out of the city and into the country. Well, we've got the place for you. This three-bedroom rural residence is just what you need. It's a spacious 3,500-square-foot, ranch-style home with a huge backyard and a pool. It's located at the end of a cul-de-sac where there are only five other homes. It is now being offered at $325,000.

CD 1, Track 10, Page 44

A. Listen to Joey and Courtney discuss two properties that Courtney looked at. As you listen, take notes about the advantages and disadvantages of each place.

Courtney: I went and looked at houses yesterday.

Joey: You did? How did it go?

Courtney: Well, I found two that I really liked. One was a three-bedroom house and the other was a two-bedroom condominium.

Joey: Which one did you like better?

Courtney: Well, they both have their plusses and minuses. The house is closer to my job than the condo, but the condo is in a much nicer neighborhood.

Joey: What about price?

Courtney: The condo is cheaper than the house, but the condo has association fees.

Joey: Did you talk to any of the people who live in the area?

Courtney: Yep. I met one of the women who lives in the condominium complex, and she looked in both neighborhoods as well when she was buying her place. She said the condominium complex is safer than the housing neighborhood because of the gate at the front. She also said that there are more children in the complex and that the neighbors seem to be friendlier because everyone lives so close together.

CD 1, Track 11, Page 45

G. Listen to Sara and Courtney talk about homes that Sara has looked at recently.

Courtney: Have you looked at any new houses this week?

Sara: Yes, I looked at three places the other day. Look at this brochure!

Courtney: The *Country Cottage*, the *Suburban Dream*, and the *Downtown Condominium*. I like the sound of the *Country Cottage* best. It sounds more comfortable than the others.

Sara: Yeah, and it's the closest to where we live now.

Courtney: Oh really? Which place is the safest?

Sara: Actually, I think the *Suburban Dream* is the safest.

Courtney: Which one has the biggest floor plan?

Sara: The *Suburban Dream*. It would be ideal for our family.

Courtney: Is it the most expensive?

Sara: Why, of course! I have expensive taste.

CD 1, Track 12, Page 47

A. Think about these questions as you listen to the story about the Bwarie family.

1. Why is the Bwarie family looking for a new home?
2. What are they looking for in a new home?

The Bwarie family has outgrown their apartment. They have three children and a baby on the way, and they are now renting a two-bedroom house. They've been putting away money every month from their paychecks, and they finally have enough money for a down payment on a house. Every Sunday, the whole family piles into the car and they go look at properties for sale. So far, they have been doing this on their own, but now it's time to find a realtor.

However, before they meet with a realtor, they need to decide exactly what they want. Courtney and Joey Bwarie have thought long and hard about what they want to purchase. First of all, they want a house in a safe neighborhood that is within walking distance to the school that their children attend. Second of all, they want four bedrooms, one for Courtney and Joey, one for the two boys, and another for their daughter and the baby girl who will be born next month. The fourth room will be used as an office for Courtney, who works out of the home. As far as bathrooms, four would be ideal, but they could survive with three if they had to. Some other things they would like are a big backyard for the children to play in and an attached two-car garage. Other amenities, such as air-conditioning or a pool, are not important to them.

Now they know what they are looking for in a new home. That was the easy part. Finding the home . . . that's a different story!

CD 1, Track 13, Page 53

B. Listen to Todd talk to the financial planner. What does the financial planner say? Is anything he says on the list you made?

Todd: I really appreciate your taking time to talk to me.

Financial Planner: No problem, Todd. I always have time for an old friend.

Todd: Well, as I told you over the phone, the boys are starting to grow up and Sara and I would like to move into a permanent place of our own. We're just a little worried about how we're going to pay for it.

Financial Planner: I think it's great that you and Sara are ready to take the next step, but only you can decide if you're ready to buy a house. Here's what I tell all my clients. First, you have to ask yourself three questions. Do you have money set aside for a down payment? Do you have enough money each month to make a loan payment? And are you ready to make a long-term financial commitment? If you can answer *yes* to all three of those questions, you are ready to buy a home.

Todd: How much will we need for a down payment?

Financial Planner: Well, that all depends on how much the house is that you want to buy. Also, you have to decide how much you want to put down. It's best if you can put 20% down, but some people can only put 5% down. The more you put down, the lower your monthly payments will be.

Todd: OK, so if we can answer *yes* to all of those questions, what's the next step?

Financial Planner: First, you need to determine how much you can afford to spend on a house. Next, you get approved for a loan for that amount. Third, start looking for a home in your price range. And fourth, make an offer on the house you want.

Todd: Looking for a home and making an offer are easy, but how do we figure out how much we can afford?

Financial Planner: The best thing to do is gather all the necessary paperwork, and then we can determine how much you can spend.

Todd: What's the necessary paperwork?

Financial Planner: I'll need six things. I'll need your social security number to run a credit check, tax statements from the past two years, two of your most recent pay stubs, the most recent statements from all your bank accounts, your most recent credit card statements, and statements from any other loans that you have. Once I have those things, I should be able to determine what your purchase price can be. If not, I'll ask you for more information.

Todd: Is there anything else I need to know?

Financial Planner: That's it for now. Why don't you and Sara sit down and discuss the three questions we talked about. If the answer is *yes* to all three, start gathering that paperwork and give me a call.

Todd: Great! Thanks for all your help.

CD 1, Track 14, Page 54

D. Listen to the first part of the conversation again. What are the three questions Todd must ask himself? Write them below.

Todd: I really appreciate your taking time to talk to me.

Financial Planner: No problem, Todd. I always have time for an old friend.

Todd: Well, as I told you over the phone, the boys are starting to grow up and Sara and I would like to move into a permanent place of our own. We're just a little worried about how we're going to pay for it.

Financial Planner: I think it's great that you and Sara are ready to take the next step, but only you can decide if you're ready to buy a house. Here's what I tell all my clients. First, you have to ask yourself three questions. Do you have money set aside for a down payment? Do you have enough money each month to make a loan payment? And are you ready to make a long-term financial commitment? If you can answer *yes* to all three of those questions, you are ready to buy a home.

Todd: How much will we need for a down payment?

Financial Planner: Well, that all depends on how much the house is that you want to buy. Also, you have to decide how much you want to put down. It's best if you can put 20% down, but some people can only put 5% down. The more you put down, the lower your monthly payments will be.

CD 1, Track 15, Page 54

E. What are the next steps Todd must take? Listen to what the financial planner says and write the four steps below.

Todd: OK, so if we can answer *yes* to all of those questions, what's the next step?

Financial Planner: First, you need to determine how much you can afford to spend on a house. Next, you get approved for a loan for that amount. Third, start looking for a home in your price range. And fourth, make an offer on the house you want.

Todd: Looking for a home and making an offer are easy, but how do we figure out how much we can afford?

Financial Planner: The best thing to do is gather all the necessary paperwork, and then we can determine how much you can spend.

CD 1, Track 16, Page 54

F. Todd will need to give the financial planner six things. Do you remember what they are? Write them below. If you can't remember, listen again.

Todd: What's the necessary paperwork?

Financial Planner: I'll need six things. I'll need your social security number to run a credit check, tax statements from the past two years, two of your most recent pay stubs, the most recent statements from all your bank accounts, your most recent credit card statements, and statements from any other loans that you have. Once I have those things, I should be able to determine what your purchase price can be. If not, I'll ask you for more information.

Todd: Is there anything else I need to know?

Financial Planner: That's it for now. Why don't you and Sara sit down and discuss the three questions we talked about. If the answer is *yes* to all three, start gathering that paperwork and give me a call.

Todd: Great! Thanks for all your help.

UNIT 4
CD 1, Track 17, Page 65
B. Listen to the phone conversations. Who did each person call? What information did he or she want?

1.
Clerk: Bay Books, how can I help you?

Caller: Um, yes, I was wondering what your store hours are?

Clerk: We're open Monday to Friday from 10 to 9 and Saturday and Sunday from 11 to 2 P.M.

Caller: Great! I think I'll stop by this afternoon.

Clerk: Is there anything in particular you're looking for?

Caller: Nope. Just want to do some browsing.

Clerk: OK! We look forward to seeing you.

Caller: Thanks. Goodbye.

Clerk: Bye.

2.
Clerk #1: Department of Motor Vehicles, this is Clarissa. How may I be of service?

Caller: I'd like to make an appointment to take a driving test.

Clerk#1: Let me transfer you to our appointment desk.

Clerk #2: Appointment desk, how can I help you?

Caller: Yes, I'd like to make an appointment to take a driving test.

Clerk #2: The next available appointment I have is on Tuesday at 3:10 P.M.

Caller: That's fine.

Clerk #2: Your name?

Caller: Peter Jones.

Clerk #2: OK, Peter. I have you down for next Tuesday the 8th at 3:10 P.M.

Caller: Thanks! See you then.

3.
Thank you for calling the Loronado Public Library. Please listen carefully to the following menu options. For our hours, press 1. For our address, press 2. For questions about our reading room, press 3. For times and dates of Children's Story Hour, press 4. For all other questions, please press 0 and you'll be connected to a librarian. Our address is 34661 Loro Road. Thank you for calling.

4.
Clerk: Computer Warehouse.

Caller: Um, yes, I was wondering if you had a certain computer in stock?

Clerk: Let me transfer you.

5.

Clerk: Hi. This is Village Elementary School. Can you please hold?
Caller: Sure.
(after a brief pause)
Clerk: Thank you for holding. How may I help you?
Caller: Yes, my name is Veronica and we just moved to Loronado from Texas.
Clerk: Wow! That's a long way!
Caller: Yes, my husband's job transferred him here.
Clerk: Well, I think you'll love Loronado.
Caller: Well, we do so far. Anyway, my son is going to be in the third grade in the fall and I need some information on how to get him registered.
Clerk: Why don't you come down to the school tomorrow morning and I'll give you all the information you need.
Caller: That would be great. Thanks!
Clerk: See you tomorrow!

CD 1, Track 18, Page 66
E. Read and listen to the conversation.
Host: Thank you for calling Scott's Steakhouse. How can I help you?
Caller: Yes, I was wondering if you are open for lunch.
Host: Yes, we are open for lunch from 11 A.M. to 3 P.M., Monday through Friday.
Caller: Do I need reservations?
Host: Reservations are not necessary, but we recommend them during the busy lunch hours.
Caller: Great. Thanks for your help!
Host: You're welcome. Goodbye.
Caller: Bye.

CD 1, Track 19, Page 68
D. Listen to the community members. Where can they find the information they need? Write the correct number next to each announcement.
1. I want to do individual exercises that will help me relax.
2. I've always wanted to learn how to play an instrument.
3. I need a place to send my kids for the summer while I'm at work.
4. Wouldn't it be fun to play on a team with other people?
5. There's gotta be something my grandmother can do Sunday nights to keep herself busy.
6. I need to find a place to live.
7. Is there a gym around here where I can play basketball?
8. I've always wanted to learn some crafts.
9. I found a lost cat in my neighborhood.

CD 1, Track 20, Page 71
D. Listen to the people giving directions. Where will the driver end up? Fill in the circle next to the correct answer.

1. Since you'll be coming from Rose, get on 24 going west. Then take 315 South. You'll drive for a while and then get off at the first exit.
2. From Grandville, get on 315 South. Then take 24 East. You'll pass the airport. Get off right before 24 and 89 intersect.
3. If you're coming from Poppington, take 315 North. Then get on 13 West, the scenic route, and go on to 15 North. You'll pass by Lake Ellie, which might be a nice place to stop and have lunch. Then continue on 15 North till you get to 315 North. Take the first exit.
4. From Rose, take 89 South until you get to the first exit. Keep going until you get to the hospital.

UNIT 5
CD 1, Track 21, Page 87
A. The doctor tells Rosa several important things about her health at her checkup. Listen and number the sentences in the correct order (1–5).
Doctor: Rosa, I can give you some more tests, but you'll have to come back in two weeks to get the results. Here's an information leaflet that tells you about exercises that will be good for your back and for your knees. If you start exercising more, your cholesterol level should go down. The fact is, if you don't stop eating junk food, you will have serious health problems. The most important thing is to stay active.

CD 1, Track 22, Page 87
B. Now listen to Rosa reporting her conversation to her friend. Fill in the missing words.
Friend: What did the doctor tell you, Rosa?
Rosa: She said she would give me some more tests.
Friend: Why? Are you very sick?
Rosa: Not now, but I might get sick. The doctor told me the most important thing was to stay active. She told me if I started exercising more, my cholesterol should go down. She said if I didn't stop eating junk food, I would have serious health problems. She said I had to come back in two weeks.

UNIT 6
CD 1, Track 23, Page 103
H. Listen to four people describe their skills, characteristics, and interests. Take notes in the first column. Then, suggest a job for each person in the second column.
1. My name is Lam and I love to be outdoors. I'm a hard worker and I like to work with my hands. I don't like to tell other people what to do, but I don't mind taking orders from my boss.
2. Hello, I'm Lilia and I love working with people. I'm very customer-service oriented and I like to help people.

I wouldn't make a good cashier because I'm not very good with numbers, but I'm willing to work hard and I learn quickly.

3. My name is Morteza and I was an engineer in my country. Unfortunately, I don't have the right qualifications to be one here, but I'm very good at technical things. I know a lot about computers and really like working with them. I prefer to work alone because I'm not very good with people.

4. Hi, I'm Hilda. I've never had a job before, but I'm very organized and good with details. I've always taken care of the finances at our house so I'm good with numbers. Also, I'm creative and like to come up with new ideas.

UNIT 7
CD 1, Track 24, Page 123
G. Listen to the tag questions. Fill in the circle next to the tag that you hear.

1. He arrived late yesterday, didn't he?
2. We'll leave early without telling the boss, won't we?
3. They didn't unload those boxes yet, did they?
4. Martina hasn't ever assembled computers, has she?
5. You're just learning how to write reports, aren't you?

CD 1, Track 25, Page 124
A. Read and listen to the conversation.

Raquel: Did you see the note I put on your screen?
Bruno: Was that note from you? I thought it was put there by Jim.
Raquel: Actually, the note was written by Jim, but I taped it to your screen. I wanted to make sure you got it before you left for lunch.
Bruno: I did get it. The orders were sent to me yesterday, and I'll have them ready for your signature before I leave today.
Raquel: Great! I'll sign them in the morning, and then you can send them to the finance department. Make sure they are sent by Package Express.
Bruno: I'll take care of it right away.

CD 1, Track 26, Page 127
A. Read and listen to the conversation.

Construction Worker: Excuse me. Do you have a second?
Supervisor: Sure. What is it?
Construction Worker: Well, there's a small problem. The shipment of lumber didn't arrive, so we have to stop construction until it gets here. What would you like us to do?
Supervisor: There's nothing else you can do while you are waiting for it?
Construction Worker: No. We need that lumber to start working on the door frames.
Supervisor: OK. Well, why don't you guys take lunch early, and I'll call and see where the lumber is?

Construction Worker: Let me make sure I understand you correctly. You want all of us to go on lunch break right now while you call and find out where the lumber is?
Supervisor: That's right.
Construction Worker: When should we come back?
Supervisor: In about an hour.
Construction Worker: Thank you. See you in an hour.

UNIT 8
CD 1, Track 27, Page 143
E. Bita telephones Consuela to ask how to get a driver's license. Listen to the conversation.

Bita: Is this Consuela?
Consuela: Yes. Who's this?
Bita: This is Bita from Bellingham, Washington.
Consuela: Hi! How are you doing?
Bita: I'm OK. A little busy with work and school, but I'm surviving. Hey, I was wondering if you could help me with something.
Consuela: Of course! What do you need?
Bita: Well, I think it's time for me to get a driver's license. Public transportation is taking up too much of my time and I need to be able to get around faster. I've been saving up to buy a car, but I still have to get my license. I remember the other day that you said you had gotten your license and registered your car, so I thought maybe you could give me some advice.
Consuela: Sure.
Bita: Well, I already have my driver's license from Iran. Do I still have to take the test?
Consuela: Yes, you'll have to take the written test and the driving test. Only people from other states in the United States can get the driving test waived.
Bita: OK, so how do I prepare for the written test?
Consuela: First, you need to go to the DMV and get a driver's handbook to study the rules of the road for the written test.
Bita: How many questions are on the test?
Consuela: In California, the written test has 36 questions. In Washington, it may be different.
Bita: How many questions do I have to get correct? And what if I don't pass it the first time?
Consuela: You can miss five questions, but you have three chances to pass the test. If you don't pass the first time, you can take it two more times.
Bita: OK. What about the driving test?
Consuela: First, you need to make an appointment. They won't let you test without one. Second, a licensed driver must accompany you to the DMV in the car that you'll use to take the test.
Bita: And then they test me on my driving skills?
Consuela: Yep.
Bita: That should be easy. I've been practicing with my brother for over a year. So, how do I apply for the license?
Consuela: First, you have to get an application and fill it out. Then you have to take the application to the DMV.
Bita: OK, so what do I have to do next?

Consuela: Well, you have to take the written test, take a vision exam, show them proof of your social security number and your date of birth, give them your thumbprint, and have your picture taken.

Bita: How much does that cost?

Consuela: $12.

Bita: OK, I think I can do this.

Consuela: I know you can. Good luck! Call me and let me know how it goes.

Bita: I sure will. Thanks a lot, Consuela!

Consuela: Anytime.

CD 1, Track 28, Page 153

A. Listen to the speeches from three people running for mayor of your city. For the first speech, put a check mark (✓) next to everything the candidate promises to do for you. For the second two speeches, write down what they promise to do for you. You will hear each speech two times.

Antonio Juliana: First of all, I want to thank you all for coming today. It is my pleasure to speak to you, and I hope that you will vote for me come Election Day. I'll be brief and to the point. My biggest concern is our streets. There is too much gang violence and I want to wipe it out. I think we can start by getting our children off the streets and taking care of the homeless people. It's time for us to regain our streets and feel safe again. Once this happens, we can focus on other problems like overcrowded schools and our public transportation system. I know you have a tough decision to make, but I hope that when you go to the polls next Tuesday, you'll put a check next to my name, Antonio Juliana.

Gary Hurt: I have been waiting for this day. A day when I could stand before you and tell you what I'm going to do if elected. These are not empty promises but things that WILL HAPPEN if you elect Gary Hurt as your mayor. The environment will be my number one priority. Our beaches will be clean again. Our public transportation system will be so good that you won't want to drive your cars anymore. I will use your tax dollars to create more parks and safe places for our children to play. Our city will be great once again if you vote for Gary Hurt!

Kwan Tan: Good evening and thank you for coming tonight! The community has given me so many opportunities and, in running for mayor, I hope to give something back to the city that welcomed me as an immigrant, educated me through my teen years, and supported me as I opened my first business.

First on my agenda is education. I will make sure your tax dollars are used to build more schools so our children won't have to sit in overcrowded classrooms. I'll lower the tuition at our community colleges so all of us will have a chance to continue and improve our education. I'll implement standards to ensure that schools are teaching our kids what they need to know. I'll start a parent-involvement program that encourages parents to participate actively in their kids' schools. Our children are the future of our community and we should invest time and money in their success.

Vote for me on Election Day and you'll have schools and a community to be proud of!

Photo Credits

UNIT 1
Page 1: Left: © M. Nader/Riser/Getty Images; Right: © Dion Ogust/The Image Works
Page 3: Top: © Dean Berry/Index Stock Imagery; Bottom: © Grantpix/Index Stock Imagery
Page 7: © Bill Lai/Index Stock Imagery
Page 8: Top: © ThinkStock LLC/Index Stock Imagery; Center: © Brad Wilson/Stone/Getty Images;
Bottom: © Inti St. Clair/Photodisc/Getty Images
Page 11: Left: © Photos.com/RF; Center: © Cindy Charles/PhotoEdit; Right: © Photos.com/RF
Page 12: © Myrleen Ferguson Cate/PhotoEdit

UNIT 3
Page 41: Left: © Comma Image/Jupiterimages; Center: © IndexOpen/RF; Right: © Royalty-Free Corbis/Jupiterimages
Page 43: Left: © Photos.com/RF; Center Left: Karl Weatherly/Photodisc/Getty Images; Center Right:
© Photos.com/RF; Right: © James Ingram/Alamy
Page 44: Top: © Thomas Northcut/Riser/Getty Images; Bottom: © Livio Sinibaldi/Photodisc/Getty Images
Page 56: Top: © Stockbyte/Getty Images; Center: © Peter Steiner/Alamy; Bottom: © Nicolas Russell/The Image Bank/
Getty Images
Page 60: Left: © IndexOpen/RF; Center: © Comma Image/Jupiterimages; Right: © Royalty-Free Corbis/Jupiterimages

UNIT 4
Page 62: © HIRB/Index Stock Imagery
Page 65: © Photos.com/RF

UNIT 5
Page 81: Left: © Bananastock/Jupiterimages; Center Left: © Seth Kushner/Jupiterimages; Center Right:
© Colin Young-Wolff/PhotoEdit; Right: © David Young-Wolff/PhotoEdit

UNIT 6
Page 103: Top: © Jeff Greenberg/PhotoEdit; Center Top: © Jeff Greenberg/PhotoEdit; Center Bottom:
© Scott Witte/Index Stock Imagery; Bottom: © Diaphor Agency/Index Stock Imagery
Page 104: © Bill Aron/PhotoEdit
Page 107: © Spencer Grant/PhotoEdit
Page 113: © IndexOpen/RF

UNIT 7
Page 127: © Dana White/PhotoEdit

UNIT 8
Page 147: Top Left: © IndexOpen/RF; Top Right: © IndexOpen/RF; Bottom Left:
© Photos.com/RF; Bottom Right: © Spencer Grant/PhotoEdit
Page 153: Top Right: © Rob Bartee/Index Stock Imagery; Center Left: © Larry George/Index Stock Imagery;
Bottom Right: © Peter Walton/Index Stock Imagery
Page 154: © Peter Walton/Index Stock Imagery

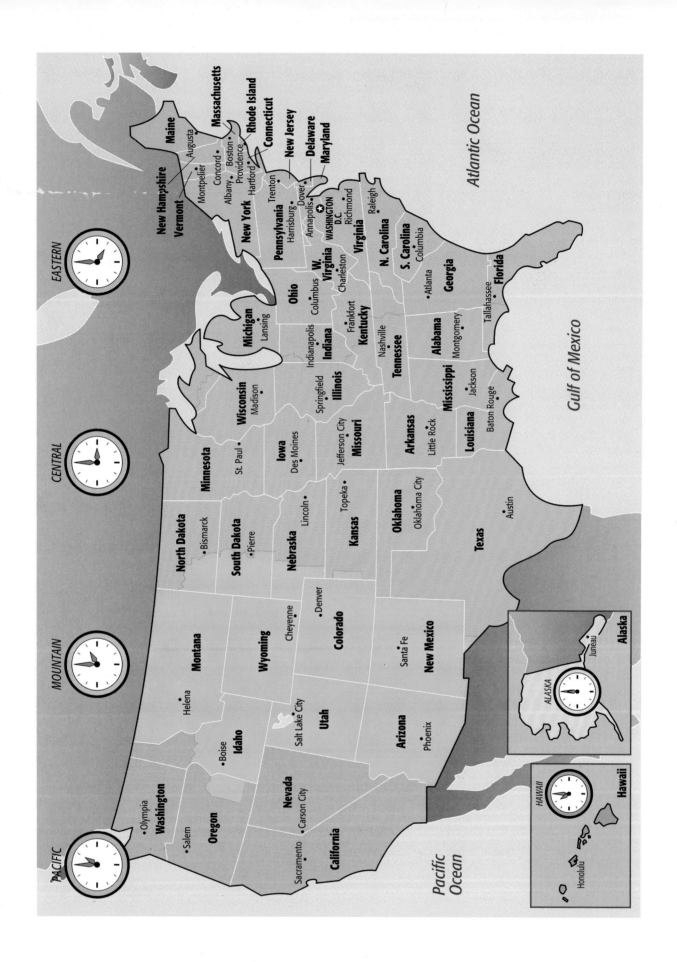